Motivating Thoughts

Swami Vivekananda

Institute of Thought & Philosophy

GRAPEVINE INDIA

Published by

GRAPEVINE INDIA PUBLISHERS PVT LTD

www.grapevineindia.com
Delhi | Mumbai
email: grapevineindiapublishers@gmail.com

Ordering Information:
Quantity sales: Special discounts are available on quantity purchases by corporations, associations, and others.
For details, reach out to the publisher.

First published by Grapevine India 2023

The mission of the Institute of Thought and Philosophy is to preserve and propagate the teachings of Swami Vivekananda. This great Indian spiritual leader is known for introducing the West to Hinduism. Drawing from his vast literary legacy, we provide valuable insights and practical guidance for modern living.

Have any query or feedback? Please reach out to us at
ITPPress123@gmail.com

A Balanced Attitude toward Work

Be perfectly resigned, perfectly unconcerned; then alone can you do any true work. No eyes can see the real forces; we can only see the results. Put out self, forget it; just let God work, it is His business.

By work alone men may get to where Buddha got largely by meditation or Christ by prayer. Buddha was a working Jnani, Christ was a Bhakta, but the same goal was reached by both of them.

Do any deserve liberty who are not ready to give it to others? Let us calmly go to work, instead of dissipating our energy in unnecessary fretting and fuming.

Each work has to pass through these stages—ridicule, opposition, and then acceptance. Those who think ahead of their time are sure to be misunderstood.

Even the greatest fool can accomplish a task if it were after his or her heart. But the intelligent ones are those who can convert every work into one that suits their taste.

No work is petty. Everything in this world is like a banyan-seed, which, though appearing tiny as a mustard-seed, has yet the gigantic banyan tree latent within it. He indeed is intelligent who notices this and succeeds in making all work truly great.

Every man who, we think, gets something by chance, has been working for it slowly and surely through ages.

In a truly noble work, not to speak of men, even God Himself befriends the doer.

It is a good discipline to be forced to work for work's sake, even to the length of not being allowed to enjoy the fruits of one's labour.

No foolish talk now, but actual work.

Not a work will be lost, no struggle vain. . .

On and on, work, work, work.

Our great defect in life is that we are so much drawn to the ideal, the goal is so much more enchanting, so much more alluring, so much bigger in our mental horizon, that we lose sight of the details altogether... One of the greatest lessons I have learnt in my life is to pay as much attention to the means of work as to its end. He was a great man from whom I learnt it, and his own life was a practical demonstration of this great principle I have been always learning great lessons from that one principle, and it appears to me that all the secret of success is there; to pay as much attention to the means as to the end.

The man who says that he will work when the world has become all good and then he will enjoy bliss is as likely to succeed as the man who sits beside the Ganga and says, "I will ford the river when all the water has run into the ocean."

The result of every work is mixed with good and evil. There is no good work that has not a touch of evil in it. Like smoke round the fire, some evil always clings to work. We should engage in such works as bring the largest amount of good and the smallest measure of evil.

The sun = Knowledge. The stormy water = Work. The lotus = Love. The serpent = Yoga. The swan = the Self. The Motto = May the Swan (the Supreme Self) send us that. It is the mind-lake.

There are certain works which are, as it were, the aggregate, the sum total, of a large number of smaller works. If we stand near the seashore and hear the waves dashing against the shingle, we think it is such a great noise, and yet we know that one wave is really composed of millions and millions of minute waves. Each one of these is making a noise, and yet we do not catch it; it is only when they become the big aggregate that we hear. Similarly, every pulsation of the heart is work. Certain kinds of work we feel and they become tangible to us; they are, at the same time, the aggregate of a number of small works. If you really want to judge of the character of a man, look not at his great performances. Every fool may become a hero at one time or another. Watch a man do his most common actions; those are indeed the things which will tell you the real character of a great man. Great occasions rouse even the lowest of human beings to some kind of greatness, but he alone is the really great man whose character is great always, the same wherever he be.

This world is not for cowards. Do not try to fly. Look not for success or failure. Join yourself to the perfectly unselfish will and work on. Know that the mind which is born to succeed joins itself to a determined will and perseveres. You have the right to work, but do not become so degenerate as to look for results. Work incessantly, but see something behind the work. Even good deeds can find a man in great bondage. Therefore be not bound by good deeds or by desire for name and fame. Those who know this secret pass beyond this round of birth and death and become immortal.

To attain liberation through work, join yourself to work but without desire, looking for no result. Such work leads to knowledge, which in turn brings emancipation. To give up work before you know, leads to misery. Work done for the Self gives no bondage. Neither desire pleasure nor fear pain from work. It is the mind and body that work, not I. Tell yourself this unceasingly and realise it. Try not to know that you work.

To work properly… you have first to give up the idea of attachment. Secondly, do not mix in the fray, hold yourself as a witness and go on working. My master used to say, "Look upon your children as a nurse does." The nurse will take your baby and fondle it and play with it and behave towards it as gently as if it were her own child; but as soon as you give her notice to quit, she is ready to start off bag and baggage from the house. Everything in the shape of attachment is forgotten.

We also read this in the Gita and learn that we have to work, constantly work with all our power; to put our whole mind in the work, whatever it be, that we are doing. At the same time, we must not be attached. That is to say, we must not be drawn away from the work by anything else; still, we must be able to quit the work whenever we like.

We read in the Bhagavad-Gita again and again that we must all work incessantly. All work is by nature composed of good and evil. We cannot do any work which will not do some good somewhere; there cannot be any work which will not cause some harm somewhere. Every work must necessarily be a mixture of good and evil; yet we are commanded to work incessantly. Good and evil will both have their results, will produce their Karma. Good action will entail upon us good effect; bad action, bad. But good and bad are both bondages of the soul. The solution reached in the Gita in regard to this bondage-producing nature of work is that, if we do not attach ourselves to the work we do, it will not have any binding effect on our soul. We shall try to understand what is meant by this "non-attachment to" to work.

When you are doing any work, do not think of anything beyond. Do it as worship.

Work and worship are necessary to take away the veil, to lift off the bondage and illusion.

Work for the idea, not the person.

Work incessantly, but be not attached to it.

Work on, brave hearts, fail not — no saying nay; work on — the Lord is behind the work. Mahashakti is with you.

Work on! Hold on! Be brave! Dare anything and everything!

Work on, my brave boys. We shall see the light some day. Let things slowly grow. Rome was not built in a day.

Work on with a heart.

Work on with energy.

Work on with the intrepidity of a lion but, at the same time with the tenderness of a flower.

Work out the salvation of this land and of the whole world, each of you thinking that the entire burden is on your shoulders.

Work through freedom! Work through love! The word "love" is very difficult to understand; love never comes until there is freedom. There is no true love possible in the slave.

Work unto death — I am with you, and when I am gone, my spirit will work with you.

Work, work — conquer all by your love!

Work, work, for, to work only for the good of others is life.

Work, work the idea, the plan, my boys, my brave, noble, good souls — to the wheel, to the wheel put your shoulders!

Work, work, work — let this be your motto.

Listen to an old story. A lazy tramp sauntering along the road saw an old man sitting at the door of his house and stopped to inquire of him the whereabouts of a certain place. "How far is such and such a village?" he asked. The old man remained silent. The man repeated his query several times. Still there was no answer. Disgusted at this, the traveller turned to go away. The old man then stood up and said, "The village of — is only a mile from here." "What!" said the tramp, "Why did you not speak when I asked you before?" "Because then", said the old man, "you seemed so halting and careless about proceeding, but now you are starting off in good earnest, and you have a right to an answer."

Will you remember this story, my son? Go to work, the rest will come: "Whosoever not trusting in anything else but Me, rests on Me, I supply him with everything he needs" (Gita, IX. 22). This is no dream.

Even the lowest forms of work are not to be despised. Let the man, who knows no better, work for selfish ends, for name and fame; but everyone should always try to get towards higher and higher motives and to understand them. "To work we have the right, but not to the fruits thereof:" Leave the fruits alone. Why care for results? If you wish to help a man, never think what that man's attitude should be towards you. If you want to do a great or a good work, do not trouble to think what the result will be.

Control Your Mind

The Being of perfect nature, universally appearing to us, is God, is Absolute. The undifferentiated is the perfect condition; all others must be lower and not permanent.

What makes the undifferentiated appear differentiated to mind? This is the same kind of question as what is the origin of evil and free will? The question itself is contradictory and impossible, because the question takes for granted cause and effect. There is no cause and effect in the undifferentiated; the question assumes that the undifferentiated is in the same condition as the differentiated.

"Whys" and "wherefores" are in mind only. The Self is beyond causation, and It alone is free. Its light it is which percolates through every form of mind. With every action I assert I am free, and yet every action proves that I am bound.

The real Self is free, yet when mixed with mind and body, It is not free. The will is the first manifestation of the real Self; the first limitation therefore of this real Self is the will. Will is a compound of Self and mind.

Now, no compound can be permanent, so that when we will to live, we must die. Immortal life is a contradiction in terms, for life, being a compound, cannot be immortal. True Being is undifferentiated and eternal.

All that is differentiated is nature. Nature is the quality of the plant, the quality of the animal, and the quality of man. Man's life behaves according to definite methods; so does his mind. Thoughts do not just happen, there is a certain method in their rise, existence and fall. In other words, just as external phenomena are bound by law, internal phenomena, that is to say, the life and mind of man, are also bound by law.

When we consider law in relation to man's mind and existence, it is at once obvious that there can be no such thing as free will and free existence. We know how animal nature is wholly regulated by law. The animal does not appear to exercise any free will. The same is true of man; human nature also is bound by law. The law governing functions of the human mind is called the law of Karma.

Nobody has ever seen anything produced out of nothing; if anything arises in the mind, that also must have been produced from something. When we speak of free will, we mean the will is not caused by anything.

But that cannot be true, the will is caused; and since it is caused, it cannot be free — it is bound by law. That I am willing to talk to you and you come to listen to me, that is law. Everything that I do or think or feel, every part of my conduct or behaviour, my every movement — all is caused and therefore not free. This regulation of our life and mind — that is the law of Karma.

If such a doctrine had been introduced in olden times into a Western community, it would have produced a tremendous commotion. The Western man does not want to think his mind is governed by law. In India it was accepted as soon as it was propounded by the most ancient Indian system of philosophy. There is no such thing as freedom of the mind; it cannot be.

The Vedas are full of passages which prove the existence of a Personal God. The Rishis, who through long devotion saw God, had a peep into the unknown and threw their challenge to the world. It is only presumptuous men, who have not walked in the path described by the Rishis and who have not followed their teachings, that criticise them and oppose them.

No man has yet come forward who would dare to say that he has properly followed their directions and has not seen anything and that these men are liars. There are men who have been under trial at various times and have felt that they have not been forsaken by God. The world is such that if faith in God does not offer us any consolation, it is better to commit suicide.

A pious missionary went out on business. All of a sudden his three sons died of cholera. His wife covered the three dead bodies of her beloved children with a sheet and was awaiting her husband at the gate.

When he returned, she detained him at the gate and put him the question, "My dear husband, some one entrusts something to you and in your absence suddenly takes it back. Will you feel sorry?" He replied, "Certainly I would not."

Then she took him in, removed the sheet and showed the three corpses. He bore this calmly and buried the bodies. Such is the strength of mind of those who hold firm faith in the existence of an all – merciful God who disposes of everything in the universe.

The Absolute can never be thought of. We can have no idea of a thing unless it is finite. God the infinite can only be conceived and worshipped as the finite.

The greatest power is lodged in the fine, not in the coarse. We see a man take up a huge weight, we see his muscles swell, and all over his body we see signs of exertion, and we think the muscles are powerful things. But it is the thin thread-like things, the nerves, which bring power to the muscles; the moment one of these threads is cut off from reaching the muscles, they are not able to work at all. These tiny nerves bring the power from something still finer, and that again in its turn brings it from something finer still — thought, and so on. So, it is the fine that is really the seat of power.

Of course we can see the movements in the gross; but when fine movements take place, we cannot see them. When a gross thing moves, we catch it, and thus we naturally identify movement with things which are gross. But all the power is really in the fine. We do not see any movement in the fine, perhaps, because the movement is so intense that we cannot perceive it.

But if by any science, any investigation, we are helped to get hold of these finer forces which are the cause of the expression, the expression itself will be under control. There is a little bubble coming from the bottom of a lake; we do not see it coming all the time, we see it only when it bursts on the surface; so, we can perceive thoughts only after they develop a great deal, or after they become actions.

We constantly complain that we have no control over our actions, over our thoughts. But how can we have it? If we can get control over the fine movements, if we can get hold of thought at the root, before it has become thought, before it has become action, then it would be possible for us to control the whole.

Now, if there is a method by which we can analyse, investigate, understand, and finally grapple with those finer powers, the finer causes, then alone is it possible to have control over ourselves, and the man who has control over his own mind assuredly will have control over every other mind. That is why purity and morality have been always the object of religion; a pure, moral man has control of himself.

And all minds are the same, different parts of one Mind. He who knows one lump of clay has known all the clay in the universe. He who knows and controls his own mind knows the secret of every mind and has power over every mind.

All these senses, external and internal, must be under the disciple's control. By hard practice he has to arrive at the stage where he can assert his mind against the senses, against the commands of nature. He should be able to say to his mind, "You are mine; I order you, do not see or hear anything", and the mind will not see or hear anything — no form or sound will react on the mind.

In that state the mind has become free of the domination of the senses, has become separated from them. No longer is it attached to the senses and the body. The external things cannot order the mind now; the mind refuses to attach itself to them. Beautiful fragrance is there.

The disciple says to the mind, "Do not smell", and the mind does not perceive the fragrance. When you have arrived at that point, you are just beginning to be a disciple. That is why when everybody says, "I know the truth", I say, "If you know the truth, you must have self-control; and if you have control of yourself, show it by controlling these organs."

Next, the mind must be made to quiet down. It is rushing about. Just as I sit down to meditate, all the vilest subjects in the world come up. The whole thing is nauseating. Why should the mind think thoughts I do not want it to think? I am as it were a slave to the mind. No spiritual knowledge is possible so long as the mind is restless and out of control. The disciple has to learn to control the mind.

Yes, it is the function of the mind to think. But it must not think if the disciple does not want it to; it must stop thinking when he commands it to. To qualify as a disciple, this state of the mind is very necessary.

Also, the disciple must have great power of endurance. Life seems comfortable; and you find the mind behaves well when everything is going well with you. But if something goes wrong, your mind loses its balance. That is not good. Bear all evil and misery without one murmur of hurt, without one thought of unhappiness, resistance, remedy, or retaliation. That is true endurance; and that you must acquire.

Good and evil there always are in the world. Many forget there is any evil — at least they try to forget; and when evil comes upon them, they are overwhelmed by it and feel bitter. There are others who deny that there is any evil at all and consider everything good. That also is a weakness; that also proceeds from a fear of evil.

If something is evil-smelling, why sprinkle it with rose water and call it fragrant? Yes, there are good and evil in the world — God has put evil in the world. But you do not have to whitewash Him. Why there is evil is none of your business. Please have faith and keep quiet.

Without the "I" there can be no "you" outside. From this some philosophers came to the conclusion that the external world did not exist save in the subject; that the "you" existed only in the "I". Others have argued that the "I" can only be known through the "you" and with equal logic. These two views are partial truths, each wrong in part and each right in part. Thought is as much material and as much in nature as body is. Both matter and mind exist in a third, a unity which divides itself into the two. This unity is the Atman, the real Self.

Give up all desire for enjoyment in earth or heaven. Control the organs of the senses and control the mind. Bear every misery without even knowing that you are miserable. Think of nothing but spiritual freedom. Have faith in Guru, in his teachings, and in the surety that you can get free. Say "Soham, Soham" whatever comes. Tell yourself this even in eating, walking, suffering; tell the mind this incessantly — that what we see never existed, that there is only "I". Flash — the dream will break! Think day and night, this universe is zero, only God is. Have intense desire to get free.

Before we can control the mind we must study it. We have to seize this unstable mind and drag it from its wanderings and fix it on one idea. Over and over again this must be done. By power of will we must get hold of the mind and make it stop and reflect upon the glory of God.

The easiest way to get hold of the mind is to sit quiet and let it drift where it will for a while. Hold fast to the idea, "I am the witness watching my mind drifting. The mind is not I." Then see it think as if it were a thing entirely apart from yourself. Identify yourself with God, never with matter or with the mind.

Picture the mind as a calm lake stretched before you and the thoughts that come and go as bubbles rising and breaking on its surface. Make no effort to control the thoughts, but watch them and follow them in imagination as they float away. This will gradually lessen the circles. For the mind ranges over wide circles of thought and those circles widen out into ever-increasing circles, as in a pond when we throw a stone into it.

We want to reverse the process and starting with a huge circle make it narrower until at last we can fix the mind on one point and make it stay there. Hold to the idea, "I am not the mind, I see that I am thinking, I am watching my mind act", and each day the identification of yourself with thought and feeling will grow less, until at last you can entirely separate yourself from the mind and actually know it to be apart from yourself.

When this is done, the mind is your servant to control as you will. The first stage of being a Yogi is to go beyond the senses. When the mind is conquered, he has reached the highest stage.

"If I know one lump of clay, I know the whole mass of clay." The universe is all built on the same plan. The individual is only a part, like the lump of clay. If we know the human soul—which is one atom—its beginning and general history, we know the whole of nature.

Birth, growth, development, decay, death—this is the sequence in all nature and is the same in the plant and the man. The difference is only in time. The whole cycle may be completed in one case in a day, in the other in three score years and ten; the methods are the same. The only way to reach a sure analysis of the universe is by the analysis of our own minds.

A proper psychology is essential to the understanding of religion. To reach Truth by reason alone is impossible, because imperfect reason cannot study its own fundamental basis. Therefore the only way to study the mind is to get at facts, and then intellect will arrange them and deduce the principles. The intellect has to build the house; but it cannot do so without bricks and it cannot make bricks. Jnana-Yoga is the surest way of arriving at facts.

We make a tremendous distinction between matter and mind; we think that the mind is entirely different from matter. Actually, they are but one nature, half of which is continually acting on the other half. Matter is pressing upon the mind in the form of various sensations. These sensations are nothing but force. The force from the outside evokes the force within. From the will to respond to or get away from the outer force, the inner force becomes what we call thought.

Both matter and mind are really nothing but forces; and if you analyse them far enough, you will find that at root they are one. The very fact that the external force can somehow evoke the internal force shows that somewhere they join each other — they must be continuous and, therefore, basically the same force. When you get to the root of things, they become simple and general.

Since the same force appears in one form as matter and in another form as mind, there is no reason to think matter and mind are different. Mind is changed into matter, matter is changed into mind. Thought force becomes nerve force, muscular force; muscular and nerve force become thought force. Nature is all this force, whether expressed as matter or mind.

The materialist frightens the idealist by claiming to derive his mind from the elements of the laboratory, while all the time he is struggling to express something higher than all elements and atoms, something of which both the external and the internal phenomena are results, and which he terms matter. The idealist, on the other hand, wants to derive all the elements and atoms of the materialist from his own thought, even while catching glimpses of something which is the cause of both mind and matter, and which he oft-times calls God. That is to say, one party wants to explain the whole universe by a portion of it which is external, the other by another portion which is internal.

Both of these attempts are impossible. Mind and matter cannot explain each other. The only explanation is to be sought for in something which will embrace both matter and mind.

Mind is cognised by the Atman, but it is not self-illuminated. The Atman cannot be the cause of anything. How can it be? How can the Purusha join itself to Prakriti (nature)? It does not; it is only illusively thought to do so….

The next point is how to use this Prana. We all use it, but how sadly we waste it! The first doctrine in the preparatory stage is that all knowledge is the outcome of experience. Whatever is beyond the five senses must also be experienced in order to become true to us.

Our mind is acting on three planes: the subconscious, conscious, and superconscious. Of men, the Yogi alone is superconscious. The whole theory of Yoga is to go beyond the mind. These three planes can be understood by considering the vibrations of light or sound. There are certain vibrations of light too slow to become visible; then as they get faster, we see them as light; and then they get too fast for us to see them at all. The same with sound.

How to transcend the senses without disturbing the health is what we want to learn. The Western mind has stumbled into acquiring some of the psychic gifts which in them are abnormal and are frequently the sign of disease. The Hindu has studied and made perfect this subject of science, which all may now study without fear or danger.

Mental healing is a fine proof of the superconscious state; for the thought which heals is a sort of vibration in the Prana, and it does not go as a thought but as something higher for which we have no name.

Each thought has three states. First, the rising or beginning, of which we are unconscious; second, when the thought rises to the surface; and third, when it goes from us. Thought is like a bubble rising to the surface. When thought is joined to will, we call it power. That which strikes the sick person whom you are trying to help is not thought, but power. The self-man running through it all is called in Sanskrit Sutratma, the "Thread-self".

The last and highest manifestation of Prana is love. The moment you have succeeded in manufacturing love out of Prana, you are free. It is the hardest and the greatest thing to gain. You must not criticise others; you must criticise yourself . If you see a drunkard, do not criticise him; remember he is you in another shape. He who has not darkness sees no darkness in others. What you have inside you is that you see in others. This is the surest way of reform. If the would-be reformers who criticise and see evil would themselves stop creating evil, the world would be better. Beat this idea into yourself.

The modern idea of nature includes only that part of the universe that is manifested on the physical plane. That which is generally understood to be mind is not considered to be nature.

Philosophers endeavouring to prove the freedom of the will have excluded the mind from nature; for as nature is bound and governed by law, strict unbending law, mind, if considered to be in nature, would be bound by law also. Such a claim would destroy the doctrine of free will; for how can that be free which is bound by law?

Law itself is the operation of cause and effect. Certain things happen according to certain other things which have gone before. Every precedent has its consequent. Thus it is in nature. If this operation of law obtains in the mind, the mind is bound and is therefore not free. No, the will is not free. How can it be? But we all know, we all feel, that one are free. Life would have no meaning, it would not be worth living, if we were not free.

The Eastern philosophers accepted this doctrine, or rather propounded it, that the mind and the will are within time, space, and causation, the same as so-called matter; and that they are therefore bound by the law of causation. We think in time; our thoughts are bound by time; all that exists, exists in time and space. All is bound by the law of causation.

That which we call matter and mind are one and the same substance. The only difference is in the degree of vibration. Mind at a very low rate of vibration is what is known as matter. Matter at a high rate of vibration is what is known as mind. Both are the same substance; and therefore, as matter is bound by time and space and causation, mind which is matter at a high rate of vibration is bound by the same law.... Mind becomes matter, and matter in its turn becomes mind, it is simply a question of vibration.

Nature is homogeneous. Differentiation is in manifestation. The Sanskrit word for nature is Prakriti, and means literally differentiation. All is one substance, but it is manifested variously.

Mind becomes matter, and matter in its turn becomes mind, it is simply a question of vibration.

Take a bar of steel and charge it with a force sufficient to cause it to vibrate, and what would happen? If this were done in a dark room, the first thing you would be aware of would be a sound, a humming sound. Increase the force, and the bar of steel would become luminous; increase it still more, and the steel would disappear altogether. It would become mind.

Take another illustration: If I do not eat for ten days, I cannot think. Only a few stray thoughts are in my mind. I am very weak and perhaps do not know my own name. Then I eat some bread, and in a little while I begin to think; my power of mind has returned. The bread has become mind. Similarly, the mind lessens its rate of vibration and manifests itself in the body, becomes matter.

As to which is first — matter or mind, let me illustrate: A hen lays an egg; the egg brings out another hen; that hen lays another egg; that egg brings out another hen, and so on in an endless chain. Now which is first — the egg or the hen? You cannot think of an egg that was not laid by a hen, or a hen that was not hatched out of an egg. It makes no difference which is first. Nearly all our ideas run themselves into the hen and egg business.

The greatest truths have been forgotten because of their very simplicity. Great truths are simple because they are of universal application. Truth itself is always simple. Complexity is due to man's ignorance.

The book one must read to learn natural sciences is the book of nature. The book from which to learn religion is your own mind and heart. The sage is often ignorant of physical science, because he reads the wrong book — the book within; and the scientist is too often ignorant of religion, because he too reads the wrong book — the book without.

Can you tell me where this "I" exists? How can you speak of anything being killed, which never exists at all? Man only remains hypnotised with the false idea of an ego. When this ghost is off from us, all dreams vanish, and then it is found that the one Self only exists from the highest Being to a blade of grass. This will have to be known, to be realised. All practice or worship is only for taking off this veil. When that will go, you will find that the Sun of Absolute Knowledge is shining in Its own lustre. For the Atman only is self-luminous and has to be realised by Itself.

How can that, which can be experienced only by itself be known with the help of any other thing? Hence the Shruti says, " — Well, through what means is that to be known which is the Knower?"

Whatever you know, you know through the instrumentality of your mind. But mind is something material. It is active only because there is the pure Self behind it. So, how can you know that Self through your mind? But this only becomes known, after all, that the mind cannot reach the pure Self, no, nor even the intellect. Our relative knowledge ends just there. Then, when the mind is free from activity or functioning, it vanishes, and the Self is revealed. This state has been described by the commentator Shankara as supersensuous perception.

Between the intellect and the grosser matter outside there is only a difference in degree. The Purusha is the only thing which is immaterial. The mind is an instrument, as it were, in the hands of the soul, through which the soul catches external objects. The mind is constantly changing and vacillating, and can, when perfected, either attach itself to several organs, to one, or to none.

For instance, if I hear the clock with great attention, I will not, perhaps, see anything although my eyes may be open, showing that the mind was not attached to the seeing organ, while it was to the hearing organ. But the perfected mind can be attached to all the organs simultaneously. It has the reflexive power of looking back into its own depths.

This reflexive power is what the Yogi wants to attain; by concentrating the powers of the mind, and turning them inward, he seeks to know what is happening inside. There is in this no question of mere belief; it is the analysis arrived at by certain philosophers.

The mind is omnipresent and can be heard and felt anywhere.

The science of Raja-Yoga proposes to give us a means of observing the internal states. The instrument is the mind itself. The power of attention, when properly guided, and directed towards the internal world, will analyse the mind, and illumine facts for us.

The powers of the mind are like rays of light dissipated; when they are concentrated, they illumine. This is our only means of knowledge. Everyone is using it, both in the external and the internal world; but, for the psychologist, the same minute observation has to be directed to the internal world, which the scientific man directs to the external; and this requires a great deal of practice.

From our childhood upwards we have been taught only to pay attention to things external, but never to things internal; hence most of us have nearly lost the faculty of observing the internal mechanism. To turn the mind as it were, inside, stop it from going outside, and then to concentrate all its powers, and throw them upon the mind itself, in order that it may know its own nature, analyse itself, is very hard work. Yet that is the only way to anything which will be a scientific approach to the subject.

The purer the mind, the easier it is to control. Purity of the mind must be insisted upon if you would control it. Do not think covetously about mere mental powers. Let them go. One who seeks the powers of the mind succumbs to them. Almost all who desire powers become ensnared by them.

Perfect morality is the all in all of complete control over mind. The man who is perfectly moral has nothing more to do; he is free. The man who is perfectly moral cannot possibly hurt anything or anybody. Non-injuring has to be attained by him who would be free. No one is more powerful than he who has attained perfect non-injuring. No one could fight, no one could quarrel, in his presence. Yes, his very presence, and nothing else, means peace, means love wherever he may be. Nobody could be angry or fight in his presence. Even the animals, ferocious animals, would be peaceful before him.

I once knew a Yogi, a very old man, who lived in a hole in the ground all by himself. All he had was a pan or two to cook his meals in. He ate very little, and wore scarcely anything, and spent most of his time meditating.

With him all people were alike. He had attained to non-injuring. What he saw in everything, in every person, in every animal, was the Soul, the Lord of the Universe. With him, every person and every animal was "my Lord". He never addressed any person or animal in any other way.

Well, one day a thief came his way and stole one of his pans. He saw him and ran after him. The chase was a long one.

At last the thief from exhaustion had to stop, and the Yogi, running up to him, fell on his knees before him and said, "My Lord, you do me a great honour to come my way. Do me the honour to accept the other pan. It is also yours."

This old man is dead now. He was full of love for everything in the world. He would have died for an ant. Wild animals instinctively knew this old man to be their friend. Snakes and ferocious animals would go into his hole and sleep with him. They all loved him and never fought in his presence.

The superconscious is the goal. Then when that state is reached, this very man becomes divine, becomes free. And to the mind thus trained to transcend all, gradually this universe will begin to give up its secrets; the book of nature will be read chapter after chapter, till the goal is attained, and we pass from this valley of life and death to that One, where death and life do not exist, and we know the Real and become the Real.

The first thing necessary is a quiet and peaceable life. If I have to go about the world the whole day to make a living, it is hard for me to attain to anything very high in this life. Perhaps in another life I shall be born under more propitious circumstances. But if I am earnest enough, these very circumstances will change even in this birth.

Was there anything you did not get which you really wanted? It could not be. For it is the want that creates the body. It is the light that has bored the holes, as it were, in your head, called the eyes. If the light had not existed, you would have had no eyes. It is sound that had made the ears. The object of perception existed first, before you made the organ. In a few hundred thousand years or earlier, we may have other organs to perceive electricity and other things.

There is no desire for a peaceful mind. Desire will not come unless there is something outside to fulfil it.

This mind is a part of the universal mind. Each mind is connected with every other mind. And each mind, wherever it is located, is in actual communication with the whole world.

The mind should always go towards God. No other things have any right to withhold it. It should continuously think of God, though this is a very hard task; yet it can be done by persistent practice. What we are now is the result of our past practice. Again, practice makes us what we shall be. So practice the other way; one sort of turning round has brought us this way, turn the other way and get out of it as soon as you can.

Thinking of the senses has brought us down here — to cry one moment, to rejoice the next, to be at the mercy of every breeze, slave to everything. This is shameful, and yet we call ourselves spirits. Go the other way, think of God; let the mind not think of any physical or mental enjoyment, but of God alone. When it tries to think of anything else, give it a good blow, so that it may turn round and think of God.

As oil poured from one vessel to another falls in an unbroken line, as chimes coming from a distance fall upon the ear as one continuous sound, so should the mind flow towards God in one continuous stream. We should not only impose this practice on the mind, but the senses too should be employed. Instead of hearing foolish things, we must hear about God; instead of talking foolish words, we must talk of God. Instead of reading foolish books, we must read good ones which tell of God.

You are not bound by law. That is in your nature. The mind is in nature and is bound by law. All nature is bound by law, the law of its own action; and this law can never be broken. If you could break a law of nature, all nature would come to an end in an instant. There would be no more nature. He who attains freedom breaks the law of nature, and for him nature fades away and has no more power over him. Each one will break the law but once and for ever; and that will end his trouble with nature.

How to Meditate

We are at the beck and call of nature. If there is sound outside, I have to hear it. If something is going on, I have to see it. Like monkeys. We are two thousand monkeys concentrated, each one of us.

Monkeys are very curious. So we cannot help ourselves, and call this "enjoying". Wonderful this language! We are enjoying the world! We cannot help enjoying it. Nature wants us to do it. A beautiful sound: I am hearing it. As if I could choose to hear it or not!

Nature says, "Go down to the depths of misery." I become miserable in a moment. We talk about pleasures of the senses and possessions.

One man thinks me very learned. Another thinks, "He is a fool." This degradation, this slavery, without knowing anything! In the dark room we are knocking our heads against each other.

What is meditation? Meditation is the power which enables us to resist all this.

Nature may call us, "Look there is a beautiful thing!" I do not look. Now she says, "There is a beautiful smell; smell it! " I say to my nose, "Do not smell it", and the nose doesn't. "Eyes, do not see!"

Nature does such an awful thing - kills one of my children, and says, "Now, rascal, sit down and weep! Go to the depths!" I say, "I don't have to." I jump up. I must be free.

Try it sometimes. In meditation, for a moment, you can change this nature. Now, if you had that power in yourself, would not that be heaven, freedom? That is the power of meditation.

Always think that this body is only an inert instrument. And the self-contained Purusha within is your real nature. The adjunct of mind is His first and subtle covering, then, there is this body which is His gross, outer covering. The indivisible changeless, self-effulgent Purusha is lying hidden under these delusive veils, therefore your real nature is unknown to you.

The direction of the mind which always runs after the senses has to be turned within. The mind has to be killed. The body is but gross — it dies and dissolves into the five elements.

But the bundle of mental impressions, which is the mind, does not die soon. It remains for some time in seed-form and then sprouts and grows in the form of a tree — it takes on another physical body and goes the round of birth and death, until Self-knowledge arises.

Therefore I say, by meditation and concentration and by the power of philosophical discrimination plunge this mind in the Ocean of Existence-Knowledge-Bliss Absolute. When the mind dies, all limiting adjuncts vanish and you are established in Brahman.

First, meditation should be of a negative nature. Think away everything. Analyse everything that comes in the mind by the sheer action of the will.

Next, assert what we really are — existence, knowledge and bliss — being, knowing, and loving.

Meditation is the means of unification of the subject and object. Meditate:

Above, it is full of me; below, it is full of me; in the middle, it is full of me. I am in all beings, and all beings are in me. Om Tat Sat, I am It. I am existence above mind. I am the one Spirit of the universe. I am neither pleasure nor pain.

The body drinks, eats, and so on. I am not the body. I am not mind. I am He.

I am the witness. I look on. When health comes I am the witness When disease comes I am the witness.

I am Existence, Knowledge, Bliss.

I am the essence and nectar of knowledge. Through eternity I change not. I am calm, resplendent, and unchanging.

Be like the pearl oyster. There is a pretty Indian fable to the effect that if it rains when the star Svati is in the ascendant, and a drop of rain falls into an oyster, that drop becomes a pearl.

The oysters know this, so they come to the surface when that star shines, and wait to catch the precious raindrop. When a drop falls into them, quickly the oysters close their shells and dive down to the bottom of the sea, there to patiently develop the drop into the pearl.

We should be like that. First hear, then understand, and then, leaving all distractions, shut your minds to outside influences, and devote yourselves to developing the truth within you.

There is the danger of frittering away your energies by taking up an idea only for its novelty, and then giving it up for another that is newer. Take one thing up and do it, and see the end of it, and before you have seen the end, do not give it up.

He who can become mad with an idea, he alone sees light. Those that only take a nibble here and a nibble there will never attain anything. They may titillate their nerves for a moment, but there it will end. They will be slaves in the hands of nature, and will never get beyond the senses.

Those who really want to be Yogis must give up, once for all, this nibbling at things. Take up one idea. Make that one idea your life — think of it, dream of it, live on that idea. Let the brain, muscles, nerves, every part of your body, be full of that idea, and just leave every other idea alone.

This is the way to success, and this is the way great spiritual giants are produced. Others are mere talking machines. If we really want to be blessed, and make others blessed, we must go deeper.

The first step is not to disturb the mind, not to associate with persons whose ideas are disturbing. All of you know that certain persons, certain places, certain foods, repel you. Avoid them; and those who want to go to the highest, must avoid all company, good or bad.

Practise hard; whether you live or die does not matter. You have to plunge in and work, without thinking of the result. If you are brave enough, in six months you will be a perfect Yogi.

But those who take up just a bit of it and a little of everything else make no progress. It is of no use simply to take a course of lessons. To those who are full of Tamas, ignorant and dull — those whose minds never get fixed on any idea, who only crave for something to amuse them — religion and philosophy are simply objects of entertainment. These are the unpersevering. They hear a talk, think it very nice, and then go home and forget all about it.

To succeed, you must have tremendous perseverance, tremendous will. "I will drink the ocean," says the persevering soul, "at my will mountains will crumble up." Have that sort of energy, that sort of will, work hard, and you will reach the goal.

There is one soul which is the greatest of all. This is Ishvara, Lord of Yoga God as Creator, with attributes. He is the individual. He is omnipotent. He resides in every heart.

There is no body. He does not need a body. All you get by the practice of meditation etc., you can get by meditation upon Ishvara, Lord of Yogis.

The same can be attained by meditating upon a great soul; or upon the harmony of life. These are called objective meditations.

So, you begin to meditate upon certain external things, objective things, either outside or inside. If you take a long sentence, that is no meditation at all. That is simply trying to get the mind collected by repetition.

Meditation means the mind is turned back upon itself. The mind stops all the thought-waves and the world stops. Your consciousness expands. Every time you meditate you will keep your growth.

Work a little harder, more and more, and meditation comes. You do not feel the body or anything else. When you come out of it after the hour, you have had the most beautiful rest you ever had in your life. That is the only way you ever give rest to your system. Not even the deepest sleep will give you such rest as that.

The mind goes on jumping even in deepest sleep. Just those few minutes in meditation your brain has almost stopped. Just a little vitality is kept up.

You may be cut to pieces and not feel it at all. You feel such pleasure in it. You become so light. This perfect rest we will get in meditation.

Meditation is a sort of prayer and prayer is meditation. The highest meditation is to think of nothing. If you can remain one moment without thought, great power will come. The whole secret of knowledge is concentration.

Soul best develops itself by loving God with all the heart. Soul is the thinking principle in man, of which mind is a function. Soul is only the conduit from Spirit to mind.

These ideas have to be understood in Dhyana, or meditation. We hear a sound. First, there is the external vibration; second, the nerve motion that carries it to the mind; third, the reaction from the mind, along with which flashes the knowledge of the object which was the external cause of these different changes from the ethereal vibrations to the mental reactions.

These three are called in Yoga, Shabda (sound), Artha (meaning), and Jnana (knowledge). In the language of physics and physiology they are called the ethereal vibration, the motion in the nerve and brain, and the mental reaction.

Now these, though distinct processes, have become mixed up in such a fashion as to become quite indistinct. In fact, we cannot now perceive any of these, we only perceive their combined effect, what we call the external object. Every act of perception includes these three, and there is no reason why we should not be able to distinguish them.

When, by the previous preparations, it becomes strong and controlled, and has the power of finer perception, the mind should be employed in meditation. This meditation must begin with gross objects and slowly rise to finer and finer, until it becomes objectless.

The mind should first be employed in perceiving the external causes of sensations, then the internal motions, and then its own reaction. When it has succeeded in perceiving the external causes of sensations by themselves, the mind will acquire the power of perceiving all fine material existences, all fine bodies and forms.

When it can succeed in perceiving the motions inside by themselves, it will gain the control of all mental waves, in itself or in others, even before they have translated themselves into physical energy; and when he will be able to perceive the mental reaction by itself, the Yogi will acquire the knowledge of everything, as every sensible object, and every thought is the result of this reaction. Then will he have seen the very foundations of his mind, and it will be under his perfect control.

Different powers will come to the Yogi, and if he yields to the temptations of any one of these, the road to his further progress will be barred. Such is the evil of running after enjoyments. But if he is strong enough to reject even these miraculous powers, he will attain to the goal of Yoga, the complete suppression of the waves in the ocean of the mind.

Then the glory of the soul, undisturbed by the distractions of the mind, or motions of the body, will shine in its full effulgence; and the Yogi will find himself as he is and as he always was, the essence of knowledge, the immortal, the all-pervading.

The power of meditation gets us everything. If you want to get power over nature, you can have it through meditation.

It is through the power of meditation all scientific facts are discovered today. They study the subject and forget everything, their own identity and everything, and then the great fact comes like a flash. Some people think that is inspiration. There is no more inspiration than there is expiration; and never was anything got for nothing.

"By constant repetition of the syllable Om and by meditating on its meaning, everything can be obtained"; "All sins are washed away by uttering the name of the Lord"; "He gets all, who resigns himself to the Will of God" — yes, these words of the Shastras and the sages are, no doubt, true.

But, do you see, thousands of us are, for our whole life, meditating on Om, are getting ecstatic in devotion in the name of the Lord, and are crying, "Thy Will be done, I am fully resigned to Thee! " — and what are they actually getting in return? Absolutely nothing!

How do you account for this? The reason lies here, and it must be fully understood.

Whose meditation is real and effective? Who can really resign himself to the Will of God? Who can utter with power irresistible, like that of a thunderbolt, the name of the Lord?

It is he who has earned Chitta-shuddhi, that is, whose mind has been purified by work, or in other words, he who is the Dharmika.

When the mind is doubtful that is not its great state. Its great state is meditation. It looks upon things and sees things, not identifying itself with anything else. As long as I feel pain, I have identified myself with the body. When I feel joy or pleasure, I have identified myself with the body.

But the high state will look with the same pleasure or blissfulness upon pleasure or upon pain. Every meditation is direct superconsciousness. In perfect concentration the soul becomes actually free from the bonds of the gross body and knows itself as it is.

Whatever one wants, that comes to him. Power and knowledge are already there. The soul identifies itself with that which is powerless matter and thus weeps. It identifies itself with mortal shapes. But if that free soul wants to exercise any power, it will have it.

If it does not, it does not come. He who has known God has become God. There is nothing impossible to such a free soul. No more birth and death for him. He is free for ever.

The greatest help to spiritual life is meditation (Dhyana). In meditation we divest ourselves of all material conditions and feel our divine nature. We do not depend upon any external help in meditation. The touch of the soul can paint the brightest colour even in the dingiest places; it can cast a fragrance over the vilest thing; it can make the wicked divine — and all enmity, all selfishness is effaced.

The less the thought of the body, the better. For it is the body that drags us down. It is attachment, identification, which makes us miserable.

That is the secret: To think that I am the spirit and not the body, and that the whole of this universe with all its relations, with all its good and all its evil, is but as a series of paintings — scenes on a canvas — of which I am the witness.

How is it to be attained? In a dozen different ways. Each temperament has its own way. But this is the general principle: get hold of the mind.

The mind is like a lake, and every stone that drops into it raises waves. These waves do not let us see what we are. The full moon is reflected in the water of the lake, but the surface is so disturbed that we do not see the reflection clearly.

Let it be calm. Do not let nature raise the wave. Keep quiet, and then after a little while she will give you up. Then we know what we are.

God is there already, but the mind is so agitated, always running after the senses. You close the senses and yet you whirl and whirl about. Just this moment I think I am all right and I will meditate upon God, and then my mind goes to London in one minute. And if I pull it away from there, it goes to New York to think about the things I have done there in the past.

These waves are to be stopped by the power of meditation. Slowly and gradually we are to train ourselves. It is no joke — not a question of a day, or years, or maybe of births.

Never mind! The pull must go on. Knowingly, voluntarily, the pull must go on. Inch by inch we will gain ground. We will begin to feel and get real possessions, which no one can take away from us — the wealth that no man can take, the wealth that nobody can destroy, the joy that no misery can hurt any more.

All these years we have depended upon others. If I have a little pleasure and that person goes away, my pleasure is gone. See the folly of man: he depends for happiness upon men! All separations are misery. Naturally. Depending upon wealth for happiness? There is fluctuation of wealth. Depending upon health or upon anything except the unchangeable spirit must bring misery today or tomorrow.

Excepting the infinite spirit, everything else is changing. There is the whirl of change. Permanence is nowhere except in yourself. There is the infinite joy, unchanging.

Meditation is the gate that opens that to us. Prayers, ceremonials, and all the other forms of worship are simply kindergartens of meditation. You pray, you offer something.

A certain theory existed that everything raised one's spiritual power. The use of certain words, flowers, images, temples, ceremonials like the waving of lights brings the mind to that attitude, but that attitude is always in the human soul, nowhere else. People are all doing it; but what they do without knowing it, do knowingly.

That is the power of meditation. All knowledge you have — how did it come? From the power of meditation. The soul churned the knowledge out of its own depths.

What knowledge was there ever outside of it? In the long run this power of meditation separates ourselves from the body, and then the soul knows itself as it is — the unborn, the deathless, and birthless being. No more is there any misery, no more births upon this earth, no more evolution. The soul knows itself as having ever been perfect and free.

Fight to Be Fit

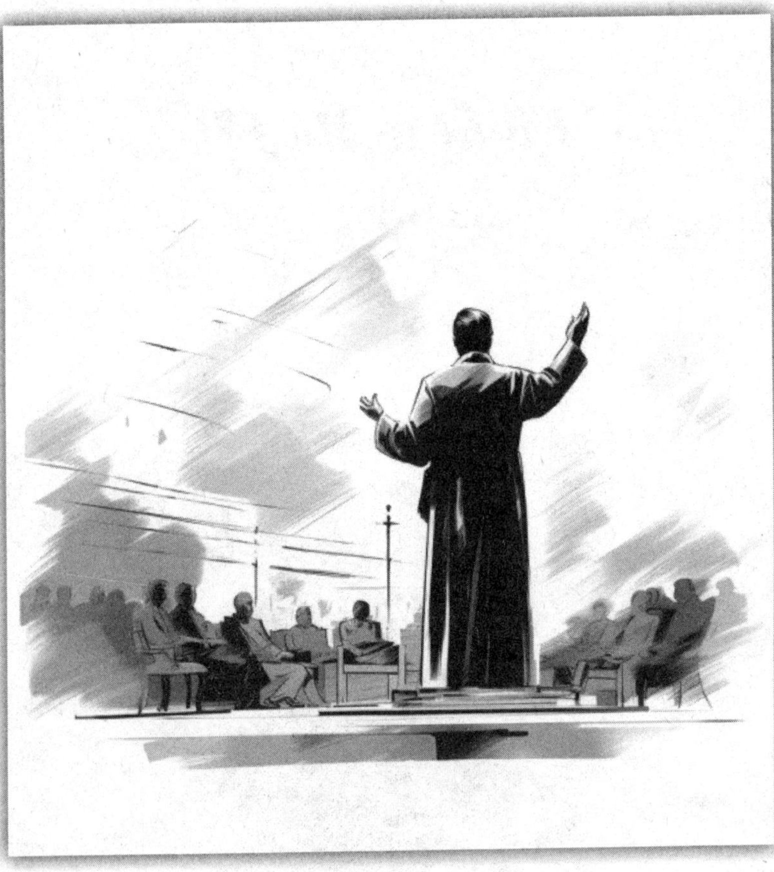

"The physically weak are unfit for the realisation of the Self." Don't you find that in a weak physique it is difficult to control the sex – appetite or anger? Lean people are quickly incensed and are quickly overcome by the sex – instinct.

Once a person gets control over the mind, it matters little whether the body remains strong or becomes emaciated. The gist of the thing is that unless one has a good physique one can never aspire to Self-realisation. Shri Ramakrishna used to say, "One fails to attain realisation if there be but a slight defect in the body".

Do you consider yourselves as men? You have got only a bit of rationality — that's all. How will you struggle with the mind unless the physique be strong? Do you deserve to be called men any longer — the highest evolution in the world? What have you got besides eating, sleeping, and satisfying the creature – comforts? Thank your stars that you have not developed into quadrupeds yet!

Shri Ramakrishna used to say, "He is the man who is conscious of his dignity".

You are but standing witnesses to the lowest class of insect – like existence of which the scripture speaks, that they simply undergo the round of births and deaths without being allowed to go to any of the higher spheres! You are simply living a life of jealousy among yourselves and are objects of hatred in the eyes of the foreigner. You are animals, therefore I recommend you to struggle.

Leave aside theories and all that. Just reflect calmly on your own everyday acts and dealings with others and find out whether you are not a species of beings intermediate between the animal and human planes of existence! First build up your own physique. Then only you can get control over the mind. "(Sanskrit)– this Self is not to be attained by the weak" (Katha Upanishad, I.ii.23).

It may be argued that early marriage leads to premature child-bearing, which accounts for most of our women dying early; their progeny also, being of low vitality, go to swell the ranks of our country's beggars!

For if the physique of the parents be not strong and healthy, how can strong and healthy children be born at all? Married a little later and bred in culture, our mothers will give birth to children who would be able to achieve the real good of the country.

The physique of this country is not at all good. If you want to do some strenuous work, it cannot bear the strain.

You must learn to make the physique very strong and teach the same to others. Don't you find me exercising every day with dumb – bells even now? Walk in the morning and evenings and do physical labour.

Body and mind must run parallel. It won't do to depend on others in everything. When the necessity of strengthening the physique is brought home to people, they will exert themselves of their own accord. It is to make them feel this need that education is necessary at the present moment.

The Importance of Concentration

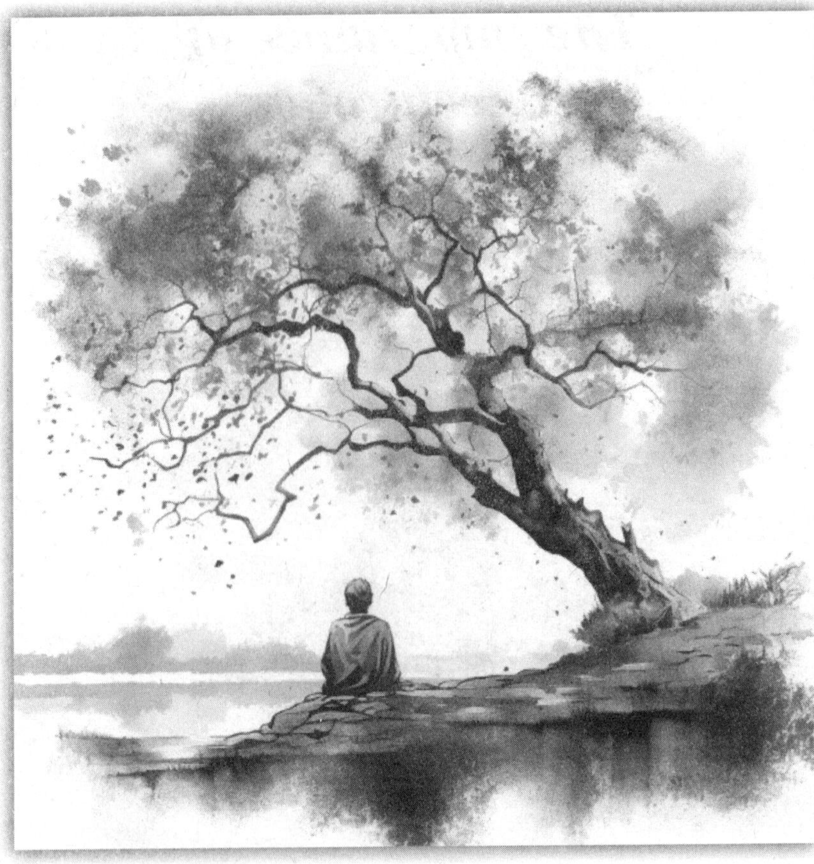

All knowledge that we have, either of the external or internal world, is obtained through only one method — by the concentration of the mind. No knowledge can be had of any science unless we can concentrate our minds upon the subject. The astronomer concentrates his mind through the telescope and so on. If you want to study your own mind, it will be the same process. You will have to concentrate your mind and turn it back upon itself. The difference in this world between mind and mind is simply the fact of concentration. One, more concentrated than the other, gets more knowledge.

Concentration is the essence of all knowledge, nothing can be done without it. Ninety per cent of thought force is wasted by the ordinary human being, and therefore he is constantly committing blunders; the trained man or mind never makes a mistake. Concentration is restraining the mind into smaller and smaller limits.

When the mind is concentrated and turned backward on itself, all within us will be our servants, not our masters. The Greeks applied their concentration to the external world, and the result was perfection in art, literature, etc. The Hindu concentrated on the internal world, upon the unseen realms in the Self, and developed the science of Yoga.

Yoga is controlling the senses, will and mind. The benefit of its study is that we learn to control instead of being controlled.

Mind seems to be layer on layer. Our real goal is to cross all these intervening strata of our being and find God. The end and aim of Yoga is to realise God.

To do this we must go beyond relative knowledge, go beyond the sense-world. The world is awake to the senses, the children of the Lord are asleep on that plane. The world is asleep to the Eternal, the children of the Lord are awake in that realm. These are the sons of God.

There is but one way to control the senses — to see Him who is the Reality in the universe. Then and only then can we really conquer our senses.

The more this power of concentration, the more knowledge is acquired, because this is the one and only method of acquiring knowledge. Even the lowest shoeblack, if he gives more concentration, will black shoes better; the cook with concentration will cook a meal all the better.

In making money, or in worshipping God, or in doing anything, the stronger the power of concentration, the better will that thing be done. This is the one call, the one knock, which opens the gates of nature, and lets out floods of light. This, the power of concentration, is the only key to the treasure-house of knowledge.

How are we to know that the mind has become concentrated? Because the idea of time will vanish. The more time passes unnoticed the more concentrated we are.

In common life we see that when we are interested in a book we do not note the time at all; and when we leave the book, we are often surprised to find how many hours have passed. All time will have the tendency to come and stand in the one present.

So the definition is given: When the past and present come and stand in one, the mind is said to be concentrated.

We read many books, but that does not bring us knowledge. We may read all the Bibles in the world, but that will not give us religion. Theoretical religion is easy enough to get, any one may get that. What we want is practical religion.

The Christian idea of a practical religion is in doing good works — worldly utility.

What good is utility? Judged from a utilitarian standpoint, religion is a failure. Every hospital is a prayer that more people may come there.

What is meant by charity? Charity is not fundamental. It is really helping on the misery of the world, not eradicating it. One looks for name and fame and covers his efforts to obtain them with the enamel of charity and good works. He is working for himself under the pretext of working for others. Every so-called charity is an encouragement of the very evil it claims to operate against.

Men and women go to balls and dance all night in honour of some hospital or other charitable institution then go home, behave like beasts, and bring devils into the world to fill jails, insane asylums, and hospitals. So it goes on, and it is called good works — building hospital etc.

The ideal of good works is to lessen, or eradicate, the misery of the world. The Yogi says, all misery comes from not being able to control the mind. The Yogi's ideal is freedom from nature. Conquest of nature is his standard of work. The Yogi says that all power is in the soul, and by the controlling of the mind and body one conquers nature by the power of the soul.

How has all the knowledge in the world been gained but by the concentration of the powers of the mind? The world is ready to give up its secrets if we only know how to knock, how to give it the necessary blow.

The strength and force of the blow come through concentration. There is no limit to the power of the human mind. The more concentrated it is, the more power is brought to bear on one point; that is the secret.

It is impossible to find God outside of ourselves. Our own souls contribute all the divinity that is outside of us. We are the greatest temple. The objectification is only a faint imitation of what we see within ourselves.

Concentration of the powers of the mind is our only instrument to help us see God. If you know one soul (your own), you know all souls, past, present, and to come.

The will concentrates the mind, certain things excite and control this will, such as reason, love, devotion, breathing. The concentrated mind is a lamp that shows us every corner of the soul.

The main difference between men and the animals is the difference in their power of concentration. All success in any line of work is the result of this.

Everybody knows something about concentration. We see its results every day. High achievements in art, music, etc., are the results of concentration.

An animal has very little power of concentration. Those who have trained animals find much difficulty in the fact that the animal is constantly forgetting what is told him. He cannot concentrate his mind long upon anything at a time. Herein is the difference between man and the animals — man has the greater power of concentration.

The difference in their power of concentration also constitutes the difference between man and man. Compare the lowest with the highest man. The difference is in the degree of concentration. This is the only difference.

Everybody's mind becomes concentrated at times. We all concentrate upon those things we love, and we love those things upon which we concentrate our minds.

What mother is there that does not love the face of her homeliest child? That face is to her the most beautiful in the world. She loves it because she concentrates her mind on it; and if every one could concentrate his mind on that same face, every one would love it. It would be to all the most beautiful face.

We all concentrate our minds upon those things we love. When we hear beautiful music, our minds become fastened upon it, and we cannot take them away. Those who concentrate their minds upon what you call classical music do not like common music, and vice versa. Music in which the notes follow each other in rapid succession holds the mind readily.

A child loves lively music, because the rapidity of the notes gives the mind no chance to wander. A man who likes common music dislikes classical music, because it is more complicated and requires a greater degree of concentration to follow it.

The great trouble with such concentrations is that we do not control the mind; it controls us. Something outside of ourselves, as it were, draws the mind into it and holds it as long as it chooses. We hear melodious tones or see a beautiful painting, and the mind is held fast! We cannot take it away.

If I speak to you well upon a subject you like, your mind becomes concentrated upon what I am saying. I draw your mind away from yourself and hold it upon the subject in spite of yourself. Thus our attention is held, our minds are concentrated upon various things, in spite of ourselves. We cannot help it.

Now the question is: Can this concentration be developed, and can we become masters of it? The Yogis say, yes. The Yogis say that we can get perfect control of the mind.

On the ethical side there is danger in the development of the power of concentration — the danger of concentrating the mind upon an object and then being unable to detach it at will. This state causes great suffering. Almost all our suffering is caused by our not having the power of detachment.

So along with the development of concentration we must develop the power of detachment. We must learn not only to attach the mind to one thing exclusively, but also to detach it at a moment's notice and place it upon something else. These two should be developed together to make it safe.

This is the systematic development of the mind. To me the very essence of education is concentration of mind, not the collecting of facts. If I had to do my education over again, and had any voice in the matter, I would not study facts at all. I would develop the power of concentration and detachment, and then with a perfect instrument I could collect facts at will. Side by side, in the child, should be developed the power of concentration and detachment.

In the lives of all great men, past and present, we find this tremendous power of concentration. Those are men of genius, you say. The science of Yoga tells us that we are all geniuses if we try hard to be. Some will come into this life better fitted and will do it quicker perhaps. We can all do the same. The same power is in everyone. The subject of the present lecture is how to concentrate the mind in order to study the mind itself. Yogis have laid down certain rules and this night I am going to give you a sketch of some of these rules.

The Practice of Concentration

Concentration, of course, comes from various sources. Through the senses you can get concentration. Some get it when they hear beautiful music, others when they see beautiful scenery. Some get concentrated by lying upon beds of spikes, sharp iron spikes, others by sitting upon sharp pebbles. These are extraordinary cases using most unscientific procedure. Scientific procedure is gradually training the mind.

One gets concentrated by holding his arm up. Torture gives him the concentration he wants. But all these are extraordinary.

Universal methods have been organised according to different philosophers. Some say the state we want to attain is super-consciousness of the mind — going beyond the limitations the body has made for us. The value of ethics to the Yogi lies in that it makes the mind pure. The purer the mind, the easier it is to control it. The mind takes every thought that rises and works it out. The grosser the mind, the more difficult it is to control it. The immoral man will never be able to concentrate his mind to study psychology. He may get a little control as he begins, get a little power of hearing. and even those powers will go from him. The difficulty is that if you study closely, you see how the extraordinary power arrived at was not attained by regular scientific training. The men who, by the power of magic, control serpents will be killed by serpents. The man who attains any extraordinary powers will in the long run succumb to those powers. There are millions who receive power through all sorts of ways in India. The vast majority of them die raving lunatics. Quite a number commit suicide, the mind being unbalanced.

The study must be put on the safe side: scientific, slow, peaceful. The first requisite is to be moral. Such a man wants the gods to come down, and they will come down and manifest themselves to him. That is our psychology and philosophy in essence, to be perfectly moral. Just think what that means! No injury, perfect purity, perfect austerity! These are absolutely necessary. Just think, if a man can attain all these in perfection! What more do you want? If he is free from all enmity towards any being, all animals will give up their enmity in his presence. The Yogis lay down very strict laws so that one cannot pass off for a charitable man without being charitable.

The law of laws is concentration. First, concentrate all the nerve energies and all power lodged in the cells of the body into one force and direct it at will. Then bring the mind, which is thinner matter, into one centre. The mind has layer after layer. When the nerve force concentrated is made to pass through the spinal column, one layer of the mind is open. When it is concentrated in one bone plexus, or "lotus", another part of the world is open. So from world to world it goes until it touches the pineal gland in the centre of the brain. This is the seat of conservation of potential energy, the source of both activity and passivity.

No one method can suit all. Different methods are not steps necessary to be taken one after another. Ceremonials are the lowest form; next God external, and after that God internal. In some cases gradation may be needed, but in many only one way is required. It would be the height of folly to say to everyone, "You must pass through Karma and Bhakti before you can reach Jnana."

Stick to your reason until you reach something higher; and you will know it to be higher, because it will not jar with reason. The stage beyond consciousness is inspiration (Samâdhi); but never mistake hysterical trances for the real thing.

It is a terrible thing to claim this inspiration falsely, to mistake instinct for inspiration. There is no external test for inspiration, we know it ourselves; our guardian against mistake is negative — the voice of reason. All religion is going beyond reason, but reason is the only guide to get there.

Instinct is like ice, reason is the water, and inspiration is the subtlest form or vapour; one follows the other. Everywhere is this eternal sequence — unconsciousness, consciousness, intelligence — matter, body, mind — and to us it seems as if the chain began with the particular link we first lay hold of. Arguments on both sides are of equal weight, and both are true. We must reach beyond both, to where there is neither the one nor the other. These successions are all Maya.

It is easy to concentrate the mind on external things, the mind naturally goes outwards; but not so in the case of religion, or psychology, or metaphysics, where the subject and the object, are one. The object is internal, the mind itself is the object, and it is necessary to study the mind itself — mind studying mind. We know that there is the power of the mind called reflection. I am talking to you. At the same time I am standing aside, as it were, a second person, and knowing and hearing what I am talking. You work and think at the same time, while a portion of your mind stands by and sees what you are thinking. The powers of the mind should be concentrated and turned back upon itself, and as the darkest places reveal their secrets before the penetrating rays of the sun, so will this concentrated mind penetrate its own innermost secrets. Thus will we come to the basis of belief, the real genuine religion. We will perceive for ourselves whether we have souls, whether life is of five minutes or of eternity, whether there is a God in the universe or more. It will all be revealed to us. This is what Raja-Yoga proposes to teach. The goal of all its teaching is how to concentrate the minds, then, how to discover the innermost recesses of our own minds, then, how to generalise their contents and form our own conclusions from them. It, therefore, never asks the question what our religion is, whether we are Deists or Atheists, whether Christians, Jews, or Buddhists. We are human beings; that is sufficient. Every human being has the right and the power to seek for religion. Every human being has the right to ask the reason, why, and to have his question answered by himself, if he only takes the trouble.

So far, then, we see that in the study of this Raja-Yoga no faith or belief is necessary. Believe nothing until you find it out for yourself; that is what it teaches us.

Do you mean to say that the facts of our awakened state require any dreams or imaginings to prove them? Certainly not. This study of Raja-Yoga takes a long time and constant practice. A part of this practice is physical, but in the main it is mental. As we proceed we shall find how intimately the mind is connected with the body. If we believe that the mind is simply a finer part of the body, and that mind acts upon the body, then it stands to reason that the body must react upon the mind. If the body is sick, the mind becomes sick also. If the body is healthy, the mind remains healthy and strong. When one is angry, the mind becomes disturbed. Similarly when the mind is disturbed, the body also becomes disturbed. With the majority of mankind the mind is greatly under the control of the body, their mind being very little developed. The vast mass of humanity is very little removed from the animals. Not only so, but in many instances, the power of control in them is little higher than that of the lower animals. We have very little command of our minds. Therefore to bring that command about, to get that control over body and mind, we must take certain physical helps. When the body is sufficiently controlled, we can attempt the manipulation of the mind. By manipulating the mind, we shall be able to bring it under our control, make it work as we like, and compel it to concentrate its powers as we desire.

Attain Divine Perfection

My ideal indeed can be put into a few words and that is: to preach unto mankind their divinity, and how to make it manifest in every movement of life.

It is an obvious fact that, with the exception of what is taken up by the necessities of life, the man of culture is loth to spend his time on so-called comforts, and even necessary actions are performed with lessened zeal, as the process moves forward. Even luxuries are arranged according to ideas and ideals, to make them reflect as much of thought-life as possible.

True love never comes until the object of our love becomes to us our highest ideal. It may be that in many cases human love is misdirected and misplaced, but to the person who loves, the thing he loves is always his own highest idea. One may see his ideal in the vilest of beings, and another in the highest of beings; nevertheless, in every case it is the ideal alone that can be truly and intensely loved.

The highest ideal of every man is called God. Ignorant or wise, saint or sinner, man or woman, educated or uneducated, cultivated or uncultivated, to every human being the highest ideal is God. The synthesis of all the highest ideals of beauty, of sublimity, and of power gives us the completest conception of the loving and lovable God.

These ideals exist in some shape or other in every mind naturally; they form a part and parcel of all our minds. All the active manifestations of human nature are struggles of those ideals to become realised in practical life. All the various movements that we see around us in society are caused by the various ideals in various souls trying to come out and become concretised; what is inside presses on to come outside.

This perennially dominant influence of the ideal is the one force, the one motive power, that may be seen to be constantly working in the midst of mankind. It may be after hundreds of births, after struggling through thousands of years, that man finds that it is vain to try to make the inner ideal mould completely the external conditions and square well with them; after realising this he no more tries to project his own ideal on the outside world, but worships the ideal itself as ideal from the highest standpoint of love.

This ideally perfect ideal embraces all lower ideals. Every one admits the truth of the saying that a lover sees Helen's beauty on an Ethiop's brow. The man who is standing aside as a looker-on sees that love is here misplaced, but the lover sees his Helen all the same and does not see the Ethiop at all. Helen or Ethiop, the objects of our love are really the centres round which our ideals become crystallised.

What is it that the world commonly worships? Not certainly this all-embracing, ideally perfect ideal of the supreme devotee and lover. That ideal which men and women commonly worship is what is in themselves; every person projects his or her own ideal on the outside world and kneels before it.

That is why we find that men who are cruel and blood-thirsty conceive of a bloodthirsty God, because they can only love their own highest ideal. That is why good men have a very high ideal of God, and their ideal is indeed so very different from that of others.

For the ordinary man and the beginner, steady devotion (Nishtha) to an ideal is of paramount importance.

It is a great thing to take up a grand ideal in life and then give up one's whole life to it. For what otherwise is the value of life, this vegetating, little, low life of man? Subordinating it to one high ideal is the only value that life has.

Everyone can see the sky, even the very worm crawling upon the earth sees the blue sky, but how very far away it is! So it is with our ideal. It is far away, no doubt, but at the same time, we know that we must have it. We must even have the highest ideal.

Unfortunately in this life, the vast majority of persons are groping through this dark life without any ideal at all. If a man with an ideal makes a thousand mistakes, I am sure that the man without an ideal makes fifty thousand.

Therefore, it is better to have an ideal. And this ideal we must hear about as much as we can, till it enters into our hearts, into our brains, into our very veins, until it tingles in every drop of our blood and permeates every pore in our body. We must meditate upon it. "Out of the fullness of the heart the mouth speaketh," and out of the fullness of the heart the hand works too.

It is knowledge that opens the door to regions of wonder, knowledge that makes a god of an animal: and that knowledge which brings us to That, "knowing which everything else is known" (the heart of all knowledge — whose pulsation brings life to all sciences — the science of religion) is certainly the highest, as it alone can make man live a complete and perfect life in thought. Blessed be the land which has styled it "supreme science"!

The principle is seldom found perfectly expressed in the practical, yet the ideal is never lost. On the one hand, it is our duty never to lose sight of the ideal, whether we can approach it with sensible steps, or crawl towards it with imperceptible motion: on the other hand, the truth is, it is always loosening in front of us — though we try our best to cover its light with our hands before our eyes.

The life of the practical is in the ideal. It is the ideal that has penetrated the whole of our lives, whether we philosophise, or perform the hard, everyday duties of life. The rays of the ideal, reflected and refracted in various straight or tortuous lines, are pouring in through every aperture and windhole, and consciously or unconsciously, every function has to be performed in its light, every object has to be seen transformed, heightened, or deformed by it.

It is the ideal that has made us what we are, and will make us what we are going to be. It is the power of the ideal that has enshrouded us, and is felt in our joys or sorrows, in our great acts or mean doings, in our virtues and vices.

If such is the power of the ideal over the practical, the practical is no less potent in forming the ideal. The truth of the ideal is in the practical. The fruition of the ideal has been through the sensing of the practical. That the ideal is there is a proof of the existence of the practical somehow, somewhere. The ideal may be vaster, yet it is the multiplication of little bits of the practical. The ideal mostly is the summed-up, generalized, practical units.

The power of the ideal is in the practical. Its work on us is in and through the practical. Through the practical, the ideal is brought down to our sense-perception, changed into a form fit for our assimilation. Of the practical we make the steps to rise to the ideal. On that we build our hopes; it gives us courage to work.

One man who manifests the ideal in his life is more powerful than legions whose words can paint it in the most beautiful colours and spin out the finest principles.

He who desires for a comfortable and nice life and at the same time wants to realise the Self is like the fool who, wanting to cross the river, caught hold of a crocodile mistaking it for a log of wood. "Seek ye first the Kingdom of God and His righteousness, and all these things shall be added unto you."

Unto him everything who does not care for anything. Fortune is like a flirt; she cares not for him who wants her, but she is at the feet of him who does not care for her. Money comes and showers itself upon one who does not care for it; so does fame come in abundance until it is a trouble and a burden.

They always come to the Master. The slave never gets anything. The Master is he who can live in spite of them, whose life does not depend upon the little, foolish things of the world. Live for an ideal, and that one ideal alone. Let it be so great, so strong, that there may be nothing else left in the mind; no place for anything else, no time for anything else.

That is the one great first step — the real desire for the ideal. Everything comes easy after that. It is not truth, but development, that is the great aim. The struggle is the great lesson. Mind you, the great benefit in this life is struggle. It is through that we pass.

If there is any road to Heaven, it is through Hell. Through Hell to Heaven is always the way. When the soul has wrestled with circumstance and has met death, a thousand times death on the way, but nothing daunted has struggled forward again and again and yet again — then the soul comes out as a giant and laughs at the ideal he has been struggling for, because he finds how much greater is he than the ideal.

I am the end, my own Self, and nothing else, for what is there to compare to me own Self? Can a bag of gold be the ideal of my Soul? Certainly not! My Soul is the highest ideal that I can have. Realising my own real nature is the one goal of my life.

The ideal man of our ancestors was the Brahmin. In all our books stands out prominently this ideal of the Brahmin.

In Europe there is my Lord the Cardinal, who is struggling hard and spending thousands of pounds to prove the nobility of his ancestors, and he will not be satisfied until he has traced his ancestry to some dreadful tyrant who lived on a hill and watched the people passing by, and whenever he had the opportunity, sprang out on them and robbed them. That was the business of these nobility-bestowing ancestors, and my Lord Cardinal is not satisfied until he can trace his ancestry to one of these.

In India, on the other hand, the greatest princes seek to trace their descent to some ancient sage who dressed in a bit of loin cloth, lived in a forest, eating roots and studying the Vedas. It is there that the Indian prince goes to trace his ancestry. You are of the high caste when you can trace your ancestry to a Rishi, and not otherwise.

Our ideal of high birth, therefore, is different from, that of others. Our ideal is the Brahmin of spiritual culture and renunciation. By the Brahmin ideal what do I mean? I mean the ideal Brahmin-ness in which worldliness is altogether absent and true wisdom is abundantly present. That is the ideal of the Hindu race.

The ideal of man is to see God in everything. But if you cannot see Him in everything, see Him in one thing, in that thing which you like best, and then see Him in another. So on you can go. There is infinite life before the soul. Take your time and you will achieve your end.

Without the supernatural sanction as it is called, or the perception of the superconscious as I prefer to term it, there can be no ethics. Without the struggle towards the Infinite there can be no ideal. Any system that wants to bind men down to the limits of their own societies is not able to find an explanation for the ethical laws of mankind.

The Utilitarian wants us to give up the struggle after the Infinite, the reaching-out for the Supersensuous, as impracticable and absurd, and, in the same breath, asks us to take up ethics and do good to society. Why should we do good? Doing good is a secondary consideration. We must have an ideal. Ethics itself is not the end, but the means to the end.

If the end is not there, why should we be ethical? Why should I do good to other men, and not injure them? If happiness is the goal of mankind, why should I not make myself happy and others unhappy? What prevents me?

In modern times, too, the attempts made to preach religions without appealing to the supersensuous state if the mind have had to take up the old abstractions of the Ancients and give different names to them as "Moral Law", the "Ideal Unity", and so forth, thus showing that these abstractions are not in the senses. None of us have yet seen an "Ideal Human Being", and yet we are told to believe in it. None of us have yet seen an ideally perfect man, and yet without that ideal we cannot progress.

Thus, this one fact stands out from all these different religions, that there is an Ideal Unit Abstraction, which is put before us, either in the form of a Person or an Impersonal Being, or a Law, or a Presence, or an Essence. We are always struggling to raise ourselves up to that ideal.

Every human being, whosoever and wheresoever he may be, has an ideal of infinite power. Every human being has an ideal of infinite pleasure. Most of the works that we find around us, the activities displayed everywhere, are due to the struggle for this infinite power or this infinite pleasure.

But a few quickly discover that although they are struggling for infinite power, it is not through the senses that it can be reached. They find out very soon that that infinite pleasure is not to be got through the senses, or, in other words, the senses are too limited, and the body is too limited, to express the Infinite.

To manifest the Infinite through the finite is impossible, and sooner or later, man learns to give up the attempt to express the Infinite through the finite. This giving up, this renunciation of the attempt, is the background of ethics. Renunciation is the very basis upon which ethics stands. There never was an ethical code preached which had not renunciation for its basis.

Two birds of beautiful plumage, inseparable companions, sat upon the same tree, one on the top and one below. The beautiful bird below was eating the fruits of the tree, sweet and bitter, one moment a sweet one and another a bitter. The moment he ate a bitter fruit, he was sorry, but after a while he ate another and when it too was bitter, he looked up and saw the other bird who ate neither the sweet nor the bitter, but was calm and majestic, immersed in his own glory.

And then the poor lower bird forgot and went on eating the sweet and bitter fruits again, until at last he ate one that was extremely bitter; and then he stopped again and once more looked up at the glorious bird above. Then he came nearer and nearer to the other bird; and when he had come near enough, rays of light shone upon him and enveloped him, and he saw he was transformed into the higher bird.

He became calm, majestic, free, and found that there had been but one bird all the time on the tree. The lower bird was but the reflection of the one above.

So we are in reality one with the Lord, but the reflection makes us seem many, as when the one sun reflects in a million dew-drops and seems a million tiny suns. The reflection must vanish if we are to identify ourselves with our real nature which is divine. The universe itself can never be the limit of our satisfaction.

That is why the miser gathers more and more money, that is why the robber robs, the sinner sins, that is why you are learning philosophy. All have one purpose. There is no other purpose in life, save to reach this freedom. Consciously or unconsciously, we are all striving for perfection. Every being must attain to it.

And what becomes of a man when he attains perfection? He lives a life of bliss infinite. He enjoys infinite and perfect bliss, having obtained the only thing in which man ought to have pleasure, namely God, and enjoys the bliss with God.

This is the common religion of all the sects of India; but, then, perfection is absolute, and the absolute cannot be two or three. It cannot have any qualities. It cannot be an individual.

And so when a soul becomes perfect and absolute, it must become one with Brahman, and it would only realise the Lord as the perfection, the reality, of its own nature and existence, the existence absolute, knowledge absolute, and bliss absolute. We have often and often read this called the losing of individuality and becoming a stock or a stone.

"He jests at scars that never felt a wound."

I tell you it is nothing of the kind. If it is happiness to enjoy the consciousness of this small body, it must be greater happiness to enjoy the consciousness of two bodies, the measure of happiness increasing with the consciousness of an increasing number of bodies, the aim, the ultimate of happiness being reached when it would become a universal consciousness.

Therefore, to gain this infinite universal individuality, this miserable little prison-individuality must go. Then alone can death cease when I am alone with life, then alone can misery cease when I am one with happiness itself, then alone can all errors cease when I am one with knowledge itself; and this is the necessary scientific conclusion.

Science has proved to me that physical individuality is a delusion, that really my body is one little continuously changing body in an unbroken ocean of matter; and Advaita (unity) is the necessary conclusion with my other counterpart, soul.

Science is nothing but the finding of unity. As soon as science would reach perfect unity, it would stop from further progress, because it would reach the goal. Thus Chemistry could not progress farther when it would discover one element out of which all other could be made. Physics would stop when it would be able to fulfil its services in discovering one energy of which all others are but manifestations, and the science of religion become perfect when it would discover Him who is the one life in a universe of death, Him who is the constant basis of an ever-changing world.

One who is the only Soul of which all souls are but delusive manifestations. Thus is it, through multiplicity and duality, that the ultimate unity is reached. Religion can go no farther. This is the goal of all science.

All science is bound to come to this conclusion in the long run. Manifestation, and not creation, is the word of science today, and the Hindu is only glad that what he has been cherishing in his bosom for ages is going to be taught in more forcible language, and with further light from the latest conclusions of science.

Descend we now from the aspirations of philosophy to the religion of the ignorant. At the very outset, I may tell you that there is no polytheism in India. In every temple, if one stands by and listens, one will find the worshippers applying all the attributes of God, including omnipresence, to the images.

It is not polytheism, nor would the name henotheism explain the situation. "The rose called by any other name would smell as sweet." Names are not explanations.

I remember, as a boy, hearing a Christian missionary preach to a crowd in India. Among other sweet things he was telling them was that if he gave a blow to their idol with his stick, what could it do? One of his hearers sharply answered, "If I abuse your God, what can He do?" "You would be punished," said the preacher, "when you die." "So my idol will punish you when you die," retorted the Hindu.

The tree is known by its fruits. When I have seen amongst them that are called idolaters, men, the like of whom in morality and spirituality and love I have never seen anywhere, I stop and ask myself, "Can sin beget holiness?"

Superstition is a great enemy of man, but bigotry is worse. Why does a Christian go to church? Why is the cross holy? Why is the face turned toward the sky in prayer? Why are there so many images in the Catholic Church? Why are there so many images in the minds of Protestants when they pray?

My brethren, we can no more think about anything without a mental image than we can live without breathing. By the law of association, the material image calls up the mental idea and vice versa.

This is why the Hindu uses an external symbol when he worships. He will tell you it helps to keep his mind fixed on the Being to whom he prays. He knows as well as you do that the image is not God, is not omnipresent.

After all, how much does omnipresence mean to almost the whole world? It stands merely as a word, a symbol. Has God superficial area? If not, when we repeat that word "omnipresent", we think of the extended sky or of space, that is all.

As we find that somehow or other, by the laws of our mental constitution, we have to associate our ideas of infinity with the image of the blue sky, or of the sea, so we naturally connect our idea of holiness with the image of a church, a mosque, or a cross. The Hindus have associated the idea of holiness, purity, truth, omnipresence, and such other ideas with different images and forms.

But with this difference that while some people devote their whole lives to their idol of a church and never rise higher, because with them religion means an intellectual assent to certain doctrines and doing good to their fellows, the whole religion of the Hindu is centred in realisation. Man is to become divine by realising the divine. Idols or temples or churches or books are only the supports, the helps, of his spiritual childhood: but on and on he must progress.

He must not stop anywhere. "External worship, material worship, "say the scriptures, "is the lowest stage; struggling to rise high, mental prayer is the next stage, but the highest stage is when the Lord has been realised."

Mark, the same earnest man who is kneeling before the idol tells you, "Him the Sun cannot express, nor the moon, nor the stars, the lightning cannot express Him, nor what we speak of as fire; through Him they shine." But he does not abuse any one's idol or call its worship sin. He recognises in it a necessary stage of life. "The child is father of the man." Would it be right for an old man to say that childhood is a sin or youth a sin?

If a man can realise his divine nature with the help of an image, would it be right to call that a sin? Nor even when he has passed that stage, should he call it an error.

To the Hindu, man is not travelling from error to truth, but from truth to truth, from lower to higher truth. To him all the religions, from the lowest fetishism to the highest absolutism, mean so many attempts of the human soul to grasp and realise the Infinite, each determined by the conditions of its birth and association, and each of these marks a stage of progress; and every soul is a young eagle soaring higher and higher, gathering more and more strength, till it reaches the Glorious Sun.

Unity in variety is the plan of nature, and the Hindu has recognised it. Every other religion lays down certain fixed dogmas, and tries to force society to adopt them. It places before society only one coat which must fit Jack and John and Henry, all alike. If it does not fit John or Henry, he must go without a coat to cover his body. The Hindus have discovered that the absolute can only be realised, or thought of, or stated, through the relative, and the images, crosses, and crescents are simply so many symbols — so many pegs to hang the spiritual ideas on. It is not that this help is necessary for every one, but those that do not need it have no right to say that it is wrong. Nor is it compulsory in Hinduism.

Religious Beliefs of the Hindu

The three essentials of Hinduism are belief in God, in the Vedas as revelation, in the doctrine of Karma and transmigration.

If one studies the Vedas between the lines, one sees a religion of harmony.

One point of difference between Hinduism and other religions is that in Hinduism we pass from truth to truth — from a lower truth to a higher truth — and never from error to truth.

The Vedas should be studied through the eye-glass of evolution. They contain the whole history of the progress of religious consciousness, until religion has reached perfection in unity.

The Vedas are Anadi, eternal. The meaning of the statement is not, as is erroneously supposed by some, that the words of the Vedas are Anadi, but that the spiritual laws inculcated by the Vedas are such. These laws which are immutable and eternal have been discovered at various times by great men or Rishis, though some of them are forgotten now, while others are preserved.

The Hindus have received their religion through revelation, the Vedas. They hold that the Vedas are without beginning and without end.

It may sound ludicrous, how a book can be without beginning or end. But by the Vedas no books are meant. They mean the accumulated treasury of spiritual laws discovered by different persons in different times. Just as the law of gravitation existed before its discovery, and would exist if all humanity forgot it, so is it with the laws that govern the spiritual world. The moral, ethical, and spiritual relations between soul and soul and between individual spirits and the Father of all spirits, were there before their discovery, and would remain even if we forgot them.

Here it may be said that these laws as laws may be without end, but they must have had a beginning. The Vedas teach us that creation is without beginning or end. Science is said to have proved that the sum total of cosmic energy is always the same. Then, if there was a time when nothing existed, where was all this manifested energy? Some say it was in a potential form in God. In that case God is sometimes potential and sometimes kinetic, which would make Him mutable. Everything mutable is a compound, and everything compound must undergo that change which is called destruction. So God would die, which is absurd. Therefore there never was a time when there was no creation.

If I may be allowed to use a simile, creation and creator are two lines, without beginning and without end, running parallel to each other. God is the ever-active providence, by whose power systems after systems are being evolved out of chaos, made to run for a time and again destroyed.

This is what the Brahmin boy repeats every day: "The sun and the moon, the Lord created like the suns and moons of previous cycles." And this agrees with modern science.

Here I stand and if I shut my eyes, and try to conceive my existence, "I", "I", "I", what is the idea before me? The idea of a body.

Am I, then, nothing but a combination of material substances? The Vedas declare, "No". I am a spirit living in a body. I am not the body. The body will die, but I shall not die. Here am I in this body; it will fall, but I shall go on living. I had also a past.

The soul was not created, for creation means a combination which means a certain future dissolution. If then the soul was created, it must die.

Some are born happy, enjoy perfect health, with beautiful body, mental vigour and all wants supplied. Others are born miserable, some are without hands or feet, others again are idiots and only drag on a wretched existence.

Why, if they are all created, why does a just and merciful God create one happy and another unhappy, why is He so partial? Nor would it mend matters in the least to hold that those who are miserable in this life will be happy in a future one. Why should a man be miserable even here in the reign of a just and merciful God?

The idea of a creator God does not explain the anomaly, but simply expresses the cruel fiat of an all-powerful being. There must have been causes, then, before his birth, to make a man miserable or happy and those were his past actions.

Are not all the tendencies of the mind and the body accounted for by inherited aptitude? Here are two parallel lines of existence — one of the mind, the other of matter. If matter and its transformations answer for all that we have, there is no necessity for supposing the existence of a soul. But it cannot be proved that thought has been evolved out of matter, and if a philosophical monism is inevitable, spiritual monism is certainly logical and no less desirable than a materialistic monism; but neither of these is necessary here.

We cannot deny that bodies acquire certain tendencies from heredity, but those tendencies only mean the physical configuration, through which a peculiar mind alone can act in a peculiar way.

There are other tendencies peculiar to a soul caused by its past actions. And a soul with a certain tendency would by the laws of affinity take birth in a body which is the fittest instrument for the display of that tendency.

This is in accord with science, for science wants to explain everything by habit, and habit is got through repetitions. So repetitions are necessary to explain the natural habits of a new-born soul. And since they were not obtained in this present life, they must have come down from past lives.

There is another suggestion. Taking all these for granted, how is it that I do not remember anything of my past life?

This can be easily explained. I am now speaking English. It is not my mother tongue, in fact no words of my mother tongue are now present in my consciousness; but let me try to bring them up, and they rush in. That shows that consciousness is only the surface of the mental ocean, and within its depths are stored up all our experiences. Try and struggle, they would come up and you would be conscious even of your past life.

This is direct and demonstrative evidence. Verification is the perfect proof of a theory, and here is the challenge thrown to the world by the Rishis. We have discovered the secret by which the very depths of the ocean of memory can be stirred up — try it and you would get a complete reminiscence of your past life.

So then the Hindu believes that he is a spirit. Him the sword cannot pierce — him the fire cannot burn — him the water cannot melt — him the air cannot dry. The Hindu believes that every soul is a circle whose circumference is nowhere, but whose centre is located in the body, and that death means the change of this centre from body to body. Nor is the soul bound by the conditions of matter. In its very essence it is free, unbounded, holy, pure, and perfect. But somehow or other it finds itself tied down to matter, and thinks of itself as matter.

Why should the free, perfect, and pure being be thus under the thraldom of matter, is the next question. How can the perfect soul be deluded into the belief that it is imperfect?

We have been told that the Hindus shirk the question and say that no such question can be there. Some thinkers want to answer it by positing one or more quasi-perfect beings, and use big scientific names to fill up the gap.

But naming is not explaining. The question remains the same. How can the perfect become the quasi-perfect; how can the pure, the absolute, change even a microscopic particle of its nature?

But the Hindu is sincere. He does not want to take shelter under sophistry. He is brave enough to face the question in a manly fashion; and his answer is: "I do not know. I do not know how the perfect being, the soul, came to think of itself as imperfect, as joined to and conditioned by matter."

But the fact is a fact for all that. It is a fact in everybody's consciousness that one thinks of oneself as the body. The Hindu does not attempt to explain why one thinks one is the body. The answer that it is the will of God is no explanation. This is nothing more than what the Hindu says, "I do not know."

Well, then, the human soul is eternal and immortal, perfect and infinite, and death means only a change of centre from one body to another. The present is determined by our past actions, and the future by the present. The soul will go on evolving up or reverting back from birth to birth and death to death.

But here is another question: Is man a tiny boat in a tempest, raised one moment on the foamy crest of a billow and dashed down into a yawning chasm the next, rolling to and fro at the mercy of good and bad actions — a powerless, helpless wreck in an ever-raging, ever-rushing, uncompromising current of cause and effect; a little moth placed under the wheel of causation which rolls on crushing everything in its way and waits not for the widow's tears or the orphan's cry?

The heart sinks at the idea, yet this is the law of Nature. Is there no hope? Is there no escape? — was the cry that went up from the bottom of the heart of despair.

It reached the throne of mercy, and words of hope and consolation came down and inspired a Vedic sage, and he stood up before the world and in trumpet voice proclaimed the glad tidings: "Hear, ye children of immortal bliss! even ye that reside in higher spheres! I have found the Ancient One who is beyond all darkness, all delusion: knowing Him alone you shall be saved from death over again."

"Children of immortal bliss" — what a sweet, what a hopeful name! Allow me to call you, brethren, by that sweet name — heirs of immortal bliss — yea, the Hindu refuses to call you sinners. Ye are the Children of God, the sharers of immortal bliss, holy and perfect beings.

Ye divinities on earth — sinners! It is a sin to call a man so; it is a standing libel on human nature. Come up, O lions, and shake off the delusion that you are sheep; you are souls immortal, spirits free, blest and eternal; ye are not matter, ye are not bodies; matter is your servant, not you the servant of matter.

Thus it is that the Vedas proclaim not a dreadful combination of unforgiving laws, not an endless prison of cause and effect, but that at the head of all these laws, in and through every particle of matter and force, stands One "by whose command the wind blows, the fire burns, the clouds rain, and death stalks upon the earth."

What is His nature?

He is everywhere, the pure and formless One, the Almighty and the All-merciful. "Thou art our father, Thou art our mother, Thou art our beloved friend, Thou art the source of all strength; give us strength. Thou art He that beareth the burdens of the universe; help me bear the little burden of this life."

Thus sang the Rishis of the Vedas. And how to worship Him? Through love. "He is to be worshipped as the one beloved, dearer than everything in this and the next life."

This is the doctrine of love declared in the Vedas, and let us see how it is fully developed and taught by Krishna, whom the Hindus believe to have been God incarnate on earth.

He taught that a man ought to live in this world like a lotus leaf, which grows in water but is never moistened by water; so a man ought to live in the world — his heart to God and his hands to work.

It is good to love God for hope of reward in this or the next world, but it is better to love God for love's sake, and the prayer goes: "Lord, I do not want wealth, nor children, nor learning. If it be Thy will, I shall go from birth to birth, but grant me this, that I may love Thee without the hope of reward — love unselfishly for love's sake."

One of the disciples of Krishna, the then Emperor of India, was driven from his kingdom by his enemies and had to take shelter with his queen in a forest in the Himalayas. There one day the queen asked him how it was that he, the most virtuous of men, should suffer so much misery.

Yudhishthira answered, "Behold, my queen, the Himalayas, how grand and beautiful they are; I love them. They do not give me anything, but my nature is to love the grand, the beautiful, therefore I love them. Similarly, I love the Lord. He is the source of all beauty, of all sublimity. He is the only object to be loved; my nature is to love Him, and therefore I love. I do not pray for anything; I do not ask for anything. Let Him place me wherever He likes. I must love Him for love's sake. I cannot trade in love."

The Vedas teach that the soul is divine, only held in the bondage of matter; perfection will be reached when this bond will burst, and the word they use for it is therefore, Mukti — freedom, freedom from the bonds of imperfection, freedom from death and misery.

And this bondage can only fall off through the mercy of God, and this mercy comes on the pure. So purity is the condition of His mercy.

How does that mercy act? He reveals Himself to the pure heart; the pure and the stainless see God, yea, even in this life; then and then only all the crookedness of the heart is made straight. Then all doubt ceases. He is no more the freak of a terrible law of causation.

This is the very centre, the very vital conception of Hinduism. The Hindu does not want to live upon words and theories. If there are existences beyond the ordinary sensuous existence, he wants to come face to face with them. If there is a soul in him which is not matter, if there is an all-merciful universal Soul, he will go to Him direct. He must see Him, and that alone can destroy all doubts.

So the best proof a Hindu sage gives about the soul, about God, is: "I have seen the soul; I have seen God." And that is the only condition of perfection. The Hindu religion does not consist in struggles and attempts to believe a certain doctrine or dogma, but in realising — not in believing, but in being and becoming.

Thus the whole object of their system is by constant struggle to become perfect, to become divine, to reach God and see God, and this reaching God, seeing God, becoming perfect even as the Father in Heaven is perfect, constitutes the religion of the Hindus.

The Immortal Soul

Let me draw your attention to one thing which unfortunately we always forget: that is — "O man, have faith in yourself." That isle the way by which we can have faith in God.

Whether you are an Advaitist or a dualist, whether you are a believer in the system of Yoga or a believer in Shankaracharya, whether you are a follower of Vyasa or Vishvamitra, it does not matter much. But the thing is that on this point Indian thought differs from that of all the rest of the world.

Let us remember for a moment that, whereas in every other religion and in every other country, the power of the soul is entirely ignored — the soul is thought of as almost powerless, weak, and inert — we in India consider the soul to be eternal and hold that it will remain perfect through all eternity. We should always bear in mind the teachings of the Upanishads.

There are certain doctrines in the Upanishads which are agreed to by all the different sects of India. First, there is the doctrine of Samsara or reincarnation of the soul. Secondly, they all agree in their psychology; first there is the body, behind that, what they call the Sukshma Sharira, the mind, and behind that even, is the Jiva.

That is the great difference between Western and Indian psychology; in the Western psychology the mind is the soul, here it is not. The Antahkarana, the internal instrument, as the mind is called, is only an instrument in the hands of that Jiva, through which the Jiva works on the body or on the external world. Here they all agree, and they all also agree that this Jiva or Atman, Jivatman as it is called by various sects, is eternal, without beginning; and that it is going from birth to birth, until it gets a final release.

They all agree in this, and they also all agree in one other most vital point, which alone marks characteristically, most prominently, most vitally, the difference between the Indian and the Western mind, and it is this, that everything is in the soul. There is no inspiration, but properly speaking, expiration. All powers and all purity and all greatness — everything is in the soul.

The Yogi would tell you that the Siddhis - Anima, Laghima, and so on — that he wants to attain to are not to be attained, in the proper sense of the word, but are already there in the soul; the work is to make them manifest. Patanjali, for instance, would tell you that even in the lowest worm that crawls under your feet, all the eightfold Yogi's powers are already existing. The difference has been made by the body. As soon as it gets a better body, the powers will become manifest, but they are there.

No search has been dearer to the human heart than that which brings to us light from God. No study has taken so much of human energy, whether in times past or present, as the study of the soul, of God, and of human destiny. However immersed we are in our daily occupations, in our ambitions, in our work, in the midst of the greatest of our struggles, sometimes there will come a pause; the mind stops and wants to know something beyond this world. Sometimes it catches glimpses of a realm beyond the senses, and a struggle to get at it is the result.

Thus it has been throughout the ages, in all countries. Man has wanted to look beyond, wanted to expand himself; and all that we call progress, evolution, has been always measured by that one search, the search for human destiny, the search for God.

What is that in man; which makes him live and move, and what becomes of that when he dies? The first philosophers studied the material substance, and tried to reach the ultimate through that. At the best, they found a personal governor of the universe, a human being immensely magnified, but yet to all intents and purposes a human being. But that could not be the whole of truth; at best, it could be only partial truth. We see this universe as human beings, and our God is our human explanation of the universe.

Suppose a cow were philosophical and had religion it would have a cow universe, and a cow solution of the problem, and it would not be possible that it should see our God. Suppose cats became philosophers, they would see a cat universe and have a cat solution of the problem of the universe, and a cat ruling it.

So we see from this that our explanation of the universe is not the whole of the solution. Neither does our conception cover the whole of the universe. It would be a great mistake to accept that tremendously selfish position which man is apt to take.

Such a solution of the universal problem as we can get from the outside labours under this difficulty that in the first place the universe we see is our own particular universe, our own view of the Reality. That Reality we cannot see through the senses; we cannot comprehend It.

Our senses are limited, very limited indeed; and within these limitations exists what we call our universe; and our God is the solution of that universe, but that cannot be the solution of the whole problem. But man cannot stop there. He is a thinking being and wants to find a solution which will comprehensively explain all the universes. He wants to see a world which is at once the world of men, and of gods, and of all possible beings, and to find a solution which will explain all phenomena.

We see, we must first find the universe which includes all universes; we must find something which, by itself, must be the material running through all these various planes of existence, whether we apprehend it through the senses or not. If we could possibly find something which we could know as the common property of the lower as well as of the higher worlds, then our problem would be solved. Even if by the sheer force of logic alone we could understand that there must be one basis of all existence, then our problem might approach to some sort of solution; but this solution certainly cannot be obtained only through the world we see and know, because it is only a partial view of the whole.

Our only hope then lies in penetrating deeper. The early thinkers discovered that the farther they were from; the centre, the more marked were the variations and differentiations; and that the nearer they approached the centre, the nearer they were to unity. The nearer we are to the centre of a circle, the nearer we are to the common ground in which all the radii meet; and the farther we are from the centre, the more divergent is our radial line from the others.

The external world is far away from the centre, and so there is no common ground in it where all the phenomena of existence can meet. At best, the external world is but one part of the whole of phenomena. There are other parts, the mental, the moral, and the intellectual — the various planes of existence — and to take up only one, and find a solution of the whole out of that one, is simply impossible.

We first, therefore, want to find somewhere a centre from which, as it were, all the other planes of existence start, and standing there we should try to find a solution. That is the proposition.

And where is that centre? It is within us. The ancient sages penetrated deeper and deeper until they found that in the innermost core of the human soul is the centre of the whole universe. All the planes gravitate towards that one point. That is the common ground, and standing there alone can we find a common solution. So the question who made this world is not very philosophical, nor does its solution amount to anything.

Everything existing has two aspects. One is noumenal, unchanging and indestructible; the other is phenomenal, changing and destructible. Man in his true nature is substance, soul, spirit. This soul, this spirit, never changes, is never destroyed; but it appears to be clothed with a form and to have a name associated with it.

This form and name are not immutable or indestructible; they continually change and are destroyed. Yet men foolishly seek immortality in this changeable aspect, in the body and mind — they want to have an eternal body. I do not want that kind of immortality.

What is the relation between me and nature? In so far as nature stands for name and form or for time, space, and causality, I am not part of nature, because I am free, I am immortal, I am unchanging and infinite. The question does not arise whether I have free will or not; I am beyond any will at all. Wherever there is will, it is never free. There is no freedom of will whatever. There is freedom of that which becomes will when name and form get hold of it, making it their slave.

That substance — the soul — as it were moulds itself, as it were throws itself into the cast of name and form, and immediately becomes bound, whereas it was free before. And yet its original nature is still there. That is why it says, "I am free; in spite of all this bondage, I am free." And it never forgets this.

But when the soul has become the will, it is no more really free. Nature pulls the strings, and it has to dance as nature wants it to. Thus have you and I danced throughout the years. All the things that we see, do, feel, know, all our thoughts and actions, are nothing but dancing to the dictates of nature. There has been, and there is, no freedom in any of this. From the lowest to the highest, all thoughts and actions are bound by law, and none of these pertain to our real Self.

My true Self is beyond all law. Be in tune with slavery, with nature, and you live under law, you are happy under law. But the more you obey nature and its dictates, the more bound you become; the more in harmony with ignorance you are, the more you are at the beck and call of everything in the universe.

Is this harmony with nature, this obedience to law, in accord with the true nature and destiny of man? What mineral ever quarrelled with and disputed any law? What tree or plant ever defied any law? This table is in harmony with nature, with law; but a table it remains always, it does not become any better.

Man begins to struggle and fight against nature. He makes many mistakes, he suffers. But eventually he conquers nature and realises his freedom. When he is free, nature becomes his slave.

The awakening of the soul to its bondage and its effort to stand up and assert itself — this is called life. Success in this struggle is called evolution. The eventual triumph, when all the slavery is blown away, is called salvation, Nirvana, freedom.

Everything in the universe is struggling for liberty. When I am bound by nature, by name and form, by time, space and causality, I do not know what I truly am. But even in this bondage my real Self is not completely lost. I strain against the bonds; one by one they break, and I become conscious of my innate grandeur.

Then comes complete liberation. I attain to the clearest and fullest consciousness of myself — I know that I am the infinite spirit, the master of nature, not its slave. Beyond all differentiation and combination, beyond space, time and causation, I am that I am.

Man's free agency is not of the mind, for that is bound. There is no freedom there. Man is not mind, he is soul. The soul is ever free, boundless, and eternal. Herein is man's freedom, in the soul. The soul is always free, but the mind identifying itself with its own ephemeral waves, loses sight of the soul and becomes lost in the maze of time, space, and causation — Maya.

This soul of man, because it is separate from the mind and body, because it is not composed of Akasha and Prana, must be immortal. Why? What do we mean by mortality? Decomposition. And that is only possible for things that are the result of composition; anything that is made of two or three ingredients must become decomposed.

That alone which is not the result of composition can never become decomposed, and, therefore, can never die. It is immortal. It has been existing throughout eternity; it is uncreate. Every item of creation is simply a composition; no one ever saw creation come out of nothing.

All that we know of creation is the combination of already existing things into newer forms. That being so, this soul of man, being simple, must have been existing for ever, and it will exist for ever. When this body falls off, the soul lives on.

According to the Vedantists, when this body dissolves, the vital forces of the man go back to his mind and the mind becomes dissolved, as it were, into the Prana, and that Prana enters into the soul of man, and the soul of man comes out, clothed, as it were, with what they call the fine body, the mental body, or spiritual body, as you may like to call it.

One thing more about the soul. Those who study the English language are often deluded by the words, soul and mind. Our Atman and soul are entirely different things. What we call Manas, the mind, the Western people call soul.

The West never had the idea of soul until they got it through Sanskrit philosophy, some twenty years ago. The body is here, beyond that is the mind, yet the mind is not the Atman; it is the fine body, the Sukshma Sharira, made of fine particles, which goes from birth to death, and so on; but behind the mind is the Atman, the soul, the Self of man.

It cannot be translated by the word soul or mind, so we have to use the word Atman, or, as Western philosophers have designated it, by the word Self. Whatever word you use, you must keep it clear in your mind that the Atman is separate from the mind, as well as from the body, and that this Atman goes through birth and death, accompanied by the mind, the Sukshma Sharira.

And when the time comes that it has attained to all knowledge and manifested itself to perfection, then this going from birth to death ceases for it. Then it is at liberty either to keep that mind, the Sukshma Sharira, or to let it go for ever, and remain independent and free throughout all eternity.

The goal of the soul is freedom. That is one peculiarity of our religion. We also have heavens and hells too; but these are not infinite, for in the very nature of things they cannot be. If there were any heavens, they would be only repetitions of this world of ours on a bigger scale, with a little more happiness and a little more enjoyment, but that is all the worse for the soul.

There are many of these heavens. Persons who do good works here with the thought of reward, when they die, are born again as gods in one of these heavens, as Indra and others. These gods are the names of certain states. They also had been men, and by good work they have become gods; and those different names that you read of, such as Indra and so on, are not the names of the same person.

There will be thousands of Indras. Nahusha was a great king, and when he died, he became Indra. It is a position; one soul becomes high and takes the Indra position and remains in it only a certain time; he then dies and is born again as man.

But the human body is the highest of all. Some of the gods may try to go higher and give up all ideas of enjoyment in heavens; but, as in this world, wealth and position and enjoyment delude the vast majority, so do most of the gods become deluded also, and after working out their good Karma, they fall down and become human beings again. This earth, therefore, is the Karma Bhumi; it is this earth from which we attain to liberation. So even these heavens are not worth attaining to.

What is then worth having? Mukti, freedom. Even in the highest of heavens, says our scripture, you are a slave; what matters it if you are a king for twenty thousand years? So long as you have a body, so long as you are a slave to happiness, so long as time works on you, space works on you, you are a slave.

The idea, therefore, is to be free of external and internal nature. Nature must fall at your feet, and you must trample on it and be free and glorious by going beyond. No more is there life; therefore more is there death. No more enjoyment; therefore no more misery. It is bliss unspeakable, in destructible, beyond everything. What we call happiness and good here are but particles of that eternal Bliss. And this eternal Bliss is our goal.

The soul is also sexless; we cannot say of the Atman that it is a man or a woman. Sex belongs to the body alone. All such ideas, therefore, as man or woman, are a delusion when spoken with regard to the Self, and are only proper when spoken of the body. So are the ideas of age. It never ages; the ancient One is always the same.

How did It come down to earth? There is but one answer to that in our scriptures. Ignorance is the cause of all this bondage. It is through ignorance that we have become bound; knowledge will cure it by taking us to the other side.

How will that knowledge come? Through love, Bhakti; by the worship of God, by loving all beings as the temples of God. He resides within them. Thus, with that intense love will come knowledge, and ignorance will disappear, the bonds will break, and the soul will be free.

According to the Vedantists, when this body dissolves, the vital forces of the man go back to his mind and the mind becomes dissolved, as it were, into the Prana, and that Prana enters into the soul of man, and the soul of man comes out, clothed, as it were, with what they call the fine body, the mental body, or spiritual body, as you may like to call it. In this body are the Samskaras of the man.

What are the Samskaras? This mind is like a lake, and every thought is like a wave upon that lake. Just as in the lake waves rise and then fall down and disappear, so these thought-waves are continually rising in the mind-stuff and then disappearing, but they do not disappear for ever. They become finer and finer, but they are all there, ready to start up at another time when called upon to do so. Memory is simply calling back into waveform some of those thoughts which have gone into that finer state of existence.

Thus, everything that we have thought, every action that we have done, is lodged in the mind; it is all there in fine form, and when a man dies, the sum total of these impressions is in the mind, which again works upon a little fine material as a medium. The soul, clothed, as it were, with these impressions and the fine body, passes out, and the destiny of the soul is guided by the resultant of all the different forces represented by the different impressions. According to us, there are three different goals for the soul.

The aspiring soul, of course, does not make out at that time that all these are external manifestations of his own mind. But all the same, there is nothing outside of it. Even what you see as this world does not exist outside. It is all a mental projection.

When the mind becomes functionless, it reflects the Brahman-consciousness. Then the vision of all spheres of existence may supervene, " — Whatsoever sphere one may call up in mind" (Mundaka, III. i. 10).

Whatsoever is resolved on becomes realised at once. He who, even on attaining this state of unfalsified self-determination, preserves his watchfulness and is free from the bondage of desire, verily attains to the knowledge of Brahman. But he who loses his balance after reaching this state gets the manifold powers, but falls off from the Supreme goal.

Those of you who have studied that most beautiful ail the Upanishads, the Katha, will remember how the king was going to make a great sacrifice, and, instead of giving away things that were of any worth, he was giving away cows and horses that were not of any use, and the book says that at that time Shraddha entered into the heart of his son Nachiketa.

I would not translate this word Shraddha to you, it would be a mistake; it is a wonderful word to understand, and much depends on it; we will see how it works, for immediately we find Nachiketa telling himself, "I am superior to many, I am inferior to few, but nowhere am I the last, I can also do something."

And this boldness increased, and the boy wanted to solve the problem which was in his mind, the problem of death. The solution could only be got by going to the house of Death, and the boy went. There he was, brave Nachiketa waiting at the house of Death for three days, and you know how he obtained what he desired. What we want, is this Shraddha.

Unfortunately, it has nearly vanished from India, and this is why we are in our present state. What makes the difference between man and man is the difference in this Shraddha and nothing else. What make one man great and another weak and low is this Shraddha. My Master used to say, he who thinks himself weak will become weak, and that is true. This Shraddha must enter into you.

Whatever of material power you see manifested by the Western races is the outcome of this Shraddha, because they believe in their muscles and if you believe in your spirit, how much more will it work! Believe in that infinite soul, the infinite power, which, with consensus of opinion, your books and sages preach.

That Atman which nothing can destroy, in It is infinite power only waiting to be called out. For here is the great difference between all other philosophies and the Indian philosophy. Whether dualistic, qualified monistic, or monistic, they all firmly believe that everything is in the soul itself; it has only to come out and manifest itself.

Therefore, this Shraddha is what I want, and what all of us here want, this faith in ourselves, and before you is the great task to get that faith. Give up the awful disease that is creeping into our national blood, that idea of ridiculing everything, that loss of seriousness. Give that up. Be strong and have this Shraddha, and everything else is bound to follow.

"What becomes of a man when the body dies ?"

"This Wise One never dies, is never born, It arises from nothing, and nothing arises from It. Unborn, Eternal, Everlasting, this Ancient One can never be destroyed with the destruction of the body. If the slayer thinks he can slay, or if the slain thinks he is slain, they both do not know the truth, for the Self neither slays nor is slain."

A most tremendous position. I should like to draw your attention to the adjective in the first line, which is "wise". As we proceed we shall find that the ideal of the Vedanta is that all wisdom and all purity are in the soul already, dimly expressed or better expressed — that is all the difference.

The difference between man and man, and all things in the whole creation, is not in kind but only in degree. The background, the reality, of everyone is that same Eternal, Ever Blessed, Ever Pure, and Ever Perfect One. It is the Atman, the Soul, in the saint and the sinner, in the happy and the miserable, in the beautiful and the ugly, in men and in animals; it is the same throughout. It is the shining One.

The difference is caused by the power of expression. In some It is expressed more, in others less, but this difference of expression has no effect upon the Atman. If in their dress one man shows more of his body than another, it does not make any difference in their bodies; the difference is in their dress.

We had better remember here that throughout the Vedanta philosophy, there is no such thing as good and bad, they are not two different things; the same thing is good or bad, and the difference is only in degree. The very thing I call pleasurable today, tomorrow under better circumstances I may call pain.

The fire that warms us can also consume us; it is not the fault of the fire. Thus, the Soul being pure and perfect, the man who does evil is giving the lie unto himself, he does not know the nature of himself. Even in the murderer the pure Soul is there; It dies not. It was his mistake; he could not manifest It; he had covered It up. Nor in the man who thinks that he is killed is the Soul killed; It is eternal. It can never be killed, never destroyed.

"Infinitely smaller than the smallest, infinitely larger than the largest, this Lord of all is present in the depths of every human heart. The sinless, bereft of all misery, see Him through the mercy of the Lord; the Bodiless, yet dwelling in the body; the Spaceless, yet seeming to occupy space; Infinite, Omnipresent: knowing such to be the Soul, the sages never are miserable."

I do not believe in eternal progress, that we are growing on ever and ever in a straight line. It is too nonsensical to believe. There is no motion in a straight line. A straight line infinitely projected becomes a circle. The force sent out will complete the circle and return to its starting place.

There is no progress in a straight line. Every soul moves in a circle, as it were, and will have to complete it; and no soul can go so low but that there will come a time when it will have to go upwards. It may start straight down, but it has to take the upward curve to complete the circuit. We are all projected from a common centre, which is God, and will come back after completing the circuit to the centre from which we started.

Each soul is a circle. The centre is where the body is, and the activity is manifested there. You are omnipresent, though you have the consciousness of being concentrated in only one point. That point has taken up particles of matter and formed them into a machine to express itself.

That through which it expresses itself is called the body. You are everywhere. When one body or machine fails you, the centre moves on and takes up other particles of matter, finer or grosser, and works through them. Here is man.

And what is God? God is a circle with circumference nowhere and centre everywhere. Every point in that circle is living, conscious, active, and equally working. With our limited souls only one point is conscious, and that point moves forward and backward.

The soul is a circle whose circumference is nowhere (limitless), but whose centre is in some body. Death is but a change of centre. God is a circle whose circumference is nowhere, and whose centre is everywhere. When we can get out of the limited centre of body, we shall realise God, our true Self.

A tremendous stream is flowing towards the ocean, carrying little bits of paper and straw hither and thither on it. They may struggle to go back, but in the long run they; must flow down to the ocean. So you and I and all nature are like these little straws carried in mad currents towards that ocean of Life, Perfection, and God. We may struggle to go back, or float against the current and play all sorts of pranks, but in the long run we must go and join this great ocean of Life and Bliss.

Each soul is potentially divine. The goal is to manifest this Divinity within, by controlling nature, external and internal. Do this either by work, or worship, or psychic control, or philosophy — by one or more or all of these — and be free. This is the whole of religion. Doctrines, or dogmas, or rituals, or books, or temples, or forms, are but secondary details.

Every soul is destined to be perfect, and every being, in the end, will attain the state of perfection. Whatever we are now is the result of our acts and thoughts in the past; and whatever we shall be in the future will be the result of what we think end do now.

But this, the shaping of our own destinies, does not preclude our receiving help from outside; nay, in the vast majority of cases such help is absolutely necessary. When it comes, the higher powers and possibilities of the soul are quickened, spiritual life is awakened, growth is animated, and man becomes holy and perfect in the end.

This quickening impulse cannot be derived from books. The soul can only receive impulses from another soul, and from nothing else. In studying books we are sometimes deluded into thinking that thereby we are being spiritually helped; but if we analyse the effect of the study of books on ourselves, we shall find that at the utmost it is only our intellect that derives profit from such studies, and not our inner spirit.

This inadequacy of books to quicken spiritual growth is the reason why, although almost every one of us can speak most wonderfully on spiritual matters, when it comes to action and the living of a truly spiritual life, we find ourselves so awfully deficient. To quicken the spirit, the impulse must come from another soul.

The person from whose soul such impulse comes is called the Guru — the teacher; and the person to whose soul the impulse is conveyed is called the Shishya — the student. To convey such an impulse to any soul, in the first place, the soul from which it proceeds must possess the power of transmitting it, as it were, to another; and in the second place, the soul to which it is transmitted must be fit to receive it.

The seed must be a living seed, and the field must be ready ploughed; and when both these conditions are fulfilled, a wonderful growth of genuine religion takes place. "The true preacher of religion has to be of wonderful capabilities, and clever shall his hearer be" — and when both of these are really wonderful and extraordinary, then will a splendid spiritual awakening result, and not otherwise.

Such alone are the real teachers, and such alone are also the real students, the real aspirants. All others are only playing with spirituality. They have just a little curiosity awakened, just a little intellectual aspiration kindled in them, but are merely standing on the outward fringe of the horizon of religion.

There is no doubt some value even in that, as it may in course of time result in the awakening of a real thirst for religion; and it is a mysterious law of nature that as soon as the field is ready, the seed must and does come; as soon as the soul earnestly desires to have religion, the transmitter of the religious force must and does appear to help that soul. When the power that attracts the light of religion in the receiving soul is full and strong, the power which answers to that attraction and sends in light does come as a matter of course.

Time begins with mind, space also is in the mind. Causation cannot stand without time. Without the idea of succession there cannot be any idea of causation. Time, space and causation, therefore, are in the mind, and as this Atman is beyond the mind and formless, it must be beyond time, beyond space, and beyond causation.

Now, if it is beyond time, space, and causation, it must be infinite. Then comes the highest speculation in our philosophy. The infinite cannot be two. If the soul be infinite, there can be only one Soul, and all ideas of various souls — you having one soul, and I having another, and so forth — are not real.

The Real Man, therefore, is one and infinite, the omnipresent Spirit. And the apparent man is only a limitation of that Real Man. In that sense the mythologies are true that the apparent man, however great he may be, is only a dim reflection of the Real Man who is beyond.

The Real Man, the Spirit, being beyond cause and effect, not bound by time and space, must, therefore, be free. He was never bound, and could not be bound. The apparent man, the reflection, is limited by time, space, and causation, and is, therefore, bound.

Or in the language of some of our philosophers, he appears to be bound, but really is not. This is the reality in our souls, this omnipresence, this spiritual nature, this infinity. Every soul is infinite, therefore there is no question of birth and death.

Some children were being examined. The examiner put them rather hard questions, and among them was this one: "Why does not the earth fall?" He wanted to evoke answers about gravitation. Most of the children could not answer at all; a few answered that it was gravitation or something. One bright little girl answered it by putting another question: "Where should it fall?"

The question is nonsense. Where should the earth fall? There is no falling or rising for the earth. In infinite space there is no up or down; that is only in the relative. Where is the going or coming for the infinite? Whence should it come and whither should it go?

Thus, when people cease to think of the past or future, when they give up the idea of body, because the body comes and goes and is limited, then they have risen to a higher ideal. The body is not the Real Man, neither is the mind, for the mind waxes and wanes. It is the Spirit beyond, which alone can live for ever.

The body and mind are continually changing, and are, in fact, only names of series of changeful phenomena, like rivers whose waters are in a constant state of flux, yet presenting the appearance of unbroken streams. Every particle in this body is continually changing; no one has the same body for many minutes together, and yet we think of it as the same body. So with the mind; one moment it is happy, another moment unhappy; one moment strong, another weak; an ever-changing whirlpool. That cannot be the Spirit which is infinite. Change can only be in the limited.

The Vedantist says that a man is neither born nor dies nor goes to heaven, and that reincarnation is really a myth with regard to the soul. The example is given of a book being turned over. It is the book that evolves, not the man. Every soul is omnipresent, so where can it come or go? These births and deaths are changes in nature which we are mistaking for changes in us.

Reincarnation is the evolution of nature and the manifestation of the God within.

The Vedanta says that each life is built upon the past, and that when we can look back over the whole past we are free. The desire to be free will take the form of a religious disposition from childhood. A few years will, as it were, make all truth clear to one. After leaving this life, and while waiting for the next, a man is still in the phenomenal.

We would describe the soul in these words: This soul the sword cannot cut, nor the spear pierce; the fire cannot burn nor water melt it; indestructible, omnipresent is this soul. Therefore weep not for it.

If it has been very bad, we believe that it will become good in the time to come. The fundamental principle is that there is eternal freedom for every one. Every one must come to it. We have to struggle, impelled by our desire to be free. Every other desire but that to be free is illusive. Every good action, the Vedantist says, is a manifestation of that freedom.

There is not one religion on the face of the earth which says that man is an improvement. The idea is that his beginning is perfect and pure, that he degenerates until he cannot degenerate further, and that there must come a time when he shoots upward again to complete the circle.

The circle must be described. However low he may go, he must ultimately take the upward bend and go back to the original source, which is God. Man comes from God in the beginning, in the middle he becomes man, and in the end he goes back to God. This is the method of putting it in the dualistic form. The monistic form is that man is God, and goes back to Him again.

If our present state is the higher one, then why is there so much horror and misery, and why is there an end to it? If this is the higher state, why does it end? That which corrupts and degenerates cannot be the highest state. Why should it be so diabolical, so unsatisfying? It is only excusable, inasmuch as through it we are taking a higher groove; we have to pass through it in order to become regenerate again.

Put a seed into the ground and it disintegrates, dissolves after a time, and out of that dissolution comes the splendid tree. Every soul must disintegrate to become God.

So it follows that the sooner we get out of this state we call "man" the better for us. Is it by committing suicide that we get out of this state? Not at all. That will be making it worse. Torturing ourselves, or condemning the world, is not the way to get out. We have to pass through the Slough of Despond, and the sooner we are through, the better. It must always be remembered that man-state is not the highest state.

You must be able to say: "I am the Soul, the ever free; I never was bound. Time is in me, not I in time. God was born in my mind. God the Father, Father of the universe — he is created by me in my own mind..

How is it that the whole world believes in going to heaven, and in dying and being born? I am studying a book, page after page is being read and turned over. Another page comes and is turned over.

Who changes? Who comes and goes? Not I, but the book. This whole nature is a book before the soul, chapter after chapter is being read and turned over, and every now and then a scene opens. That is read and turned over. A fresh one comes, but the soul is ever the same — eternal. It is nature that is changing, not the soul of man. This never changes.

Birth and death are in nature, not in you. Yet the ignorant are deluded; just as we under delusion think that the sun is moving and not the earth, in exactly the same way we think that we are dying, and not nature. These are all, therefore, hallucinations. Just as it is a hallucination when we think that the fields are moving and not the railway train, exactly in the same manner is the hallucination of birth and death.

The soul is beyond all laws, physical, mental, or moral.

Sometimes I have young men come and talk to me about atheism; I do not believe a Hindu can become an atheist. He may read European books, and persuade himself he is a materialist, but it is only for a time. It is not in your blood. You cannot believe what is not in your constitution; it would be a hopeless task for you.

Do not attempt that sort of thing. I once attempted it when I was a boy, but it could not be. Life is short, but the soul is immortal and eternal, and one thing being certain, death, let us therefore take up a great ideal and give up our whole life to it.

Let this be our determination, and may He, the Lord, who "comes again and again for the salvation of His own people", to quote from our scriptures — may the great Krishna bless us and lead us all to the fulfilment of our aims!

If the others are not born clever, let them have all the teaching and the teachers they want. This is justice and reason as I understand it. Our poor people, these downtrodden masses of India, therefore, require to hear and to know what they really are.

Ay, let every man and woman and child, without respect of caste or birth, weakness or strength, hear and learn that behind the strong and the weak, behind the high and the low, behind every one, there is that Infinite Soul, assuring the infinite possibility and the infinite capacity of all to become great and good. Let us proclaim to every soul: — Arise, awake, and stop not till the goal is reached.

Arise, awake! Awake from this hypnotism of weakness. None is really weak; the soul is infinite, omnipotent, and omniscient. Stand up, assert yourself, proclaim the God within you, do not deny Him! Too much of inactivity, too much of weakness, too much of hypnotism has been and is upon our race.

O ye modern Hindus, de-hypnotise yourselves. The way to do that is found in your own sacred books. Teach yourselves, teach every one his real nature, call upon the sleeping soul and see how it awakes. Power will come, glory will come, goodness will come, purity will come, and everything that is excellent will come when this sleeping soul is roused to self-conscious activity.

Ay, if there is anything in the Gita that I like, it is these two verses, coming out strong as the very gist, the very essence, of Krishna's teaching — "He who sees the Supreme Lord dwelling alike in all beings, the Imperishable in things that perish, he sees indeed. For seeing the Lord as the same, everywhere present, he does not destroy the Self by the Self, and thus he goes to the highest goal."

Everything that is a compound must sooner or later go back to its component parts. Whatever in this universe is the result of the combination of matter or force must sooner or later go back to its components. Whatever is the result of certain causes must die, must be destroyed. It gets broken up, dispersed, and resolved back into its components.

Soul is not a force; neither is it thought. It is the manufacturer of thought, but not thought itself; it is the manufacturer of the body, but not the body.

Why so? We see that the body cannot be the soul. Why not? Because it is not intelligent. A corpse is not intelligent, nor a piece of meat in a butcher's shop. What do we mean by intelligence? Reactive power.

We want to go a little more deeply into this. Here is a pitcher; I see it. How? Rays of light from the pitcher enter my eyes, and make a picture in my retina, which is carried to the brain.

Yet there is no vision. What the physiologists call the sensory nerves carry this impression inwards. But up to this there is no reaction. The nerve centre in the brain carries the impression to the mind, and the mind reacts, and as soon as this reaction comes, the pitcher flashes before it.

When a new impression comes, if the mind does not react, we shall not be conscious of it, but when the reaction comes we feel, we see, we hear, and so forth. With this reaction comes illumination, as the Samkhya philosophers call it. We see that the body cannot illuminate, because in the absence of attention no sensation is possible.

Cases have been known where, under peculiar conditions, a man who had never learnt a particular language was found able to speak it. Subsequent inquiries proved that the man had, when a child, lived among people who spoke that language and the impressions were left in his brain. These impressions remained stored up there, until through some cause the mind reacted, and illumination came, and then the man was able to speak the language. The mind alone is not sufficient, that the mind itself is an instrument in the hands of someone.

In the case of that boy the mind contained that language, yet he did not know it, but later there came a time when he did. It shows that there is someone besides the mind; and when the boy was a baby, that someone did not use the power; but when the boy grew up, he took advantage of it, and used it.

First, here is the body, second the mind, or instrument of thought, and third behind this mind is the Self of man. The Sanskrit word is Atman. As modern philosophers have identified thought with molecular changes in the brain, they do not know how to explain such a case, and they generally deny it.

The mind is intimately connected with the brain which dies every time the body changes. The Self is the illuminator, and the mind is the instrument in Its hands, and through that instrument It gets hold of the external instrument, and thus comes perception. The external instruments get hold of the impressions and carry them to the organs, for you must remember always, that the eyes and ears are only receivers — it is the internal organs, the brain centres, which act.

In Sanskrit these centres are called Indriyas, and they carry sensations to the mind, and the mind presents them further back to another state of the mind, which in Sanskrit is called Chitta, and there they are organised into will, and all these present them to the King of kings inside, the Ruler on His throne, the Self of man. He then sees and gives His orders.

Then the mind immediately acts on the organs, and the organs on the external body. The real Perceiver, the real Ruler, the Governor, the Creator, the Manipulator of all this, is the Self of man.

We see, then, that the Self of man is not the body, neither is It thought. It cannot be a compound.

Why not? Because everything that is a compound can be seen or imagined. That which we cannot imagine or perceive, which we cannot bind together, is not force or matter, cause or effect, and cannot be a compound. The domain of compounds is only so far as our mental universe, our thought universe extends. Beyond this it does not hold good; it is as far as law reigns, and if there is anything beyond law, it cannot be a compound at all.

The Self of man being beyond the law of causation, is not a compound. It is ever free and is the Ruler of everything that is within law. It will never die, because death means going back to the component parts, and that which was never a compound can never die. It is sheer nonsense to say It dies.

The misery that we suffer comes from ignorance, from non-discrimination between the real and the unreal. We all take the bad for the good, the dream for the reality. Soul is the only reality, and we have forgotten it. Body is an unreal dream, and we think we are all bodies.

This non-discrimination is the cause of misery. It is caused by ignorance. When discrimination comes, it brings strength, and then alone can we avoid all these various ideas of body, heavens, and gods.

This ignorance arises through differentiating by species, sign, and place. For instance, take a cow. The cow is differentiated from the dog by species.

Even with the cows alone how do we make the distinction between one cow and another? By signs. If two objects are exactly similar, they can be distinguished if they are in different places. When objects are so mixed up that even these differential will not help us, the power of discrimination acquired by the above-mentioned practice will give us the ability to distinguish them.

The highest philosophy of the Yogi is based upon this fact, that the Purusha is pure and perfect, and is the only "simple" that exists in this universe. The body and mind are compounds, and yet we are ever identifying ourselves with them This is the great mistake that the distinction has been lost. When this power of discrimination has been attained, man sees that everything in this world, mental and physical, is a compound, and, as such, cannot be the Purusha.

Various heavens are spoken of in the Brahmana portions of the Vedas, but the philosophical teaching of the Upanishads gives up the idea of going to heaven. Happiness is not in this heaven or in that heaven, it is in the soul; places do not signify anything.

Here is another passage which shows the different states of realisation. "In the heaven of the forefathers, as a man sees things in a dream, so the Real Truth is seen."

As in dreams we see things hazy and not so distinct, so we see the Reality there. There is another heaven called the Gandharva, in which it is still less clear; as a man sees his own reflection in the water, so is the Reality seen there.

The highest heaven, of which the Hindus conceive is called the Brahmaloka; and in this, the Truth is seen much more clearly, like light and shade, but not yet quite distinctly. But as a man sees his own face in a mirror, perfect, distinct, and clear, so is the Truth shining in the soul of man.

The highest heaven, therefore, is in our own souls; the greatest temple of worship is the human soul, greater than all heavens, says the Vedanta; for in no heaven anywhere, can we understand the reality as distinctly and clearly as in this life, in our own soul.

Knowledge is not to be acquired from without. It is the innate nature of the human soul and the essential birthright of every man. The human soul is the repository of infinite wisdom; what external agency can illuminate it?

The pain-bearing obstructions are — ignorance, egoism, attachment, aversion and clinging to life.

These are the five pains, the fivefold tie that binds us down, of which ignorance is the cause and the other four its effects. It is the only cause of all our misery. What else can make us miserable? The nature of the Soul is eternal bliss. What can make it sorrowful except ignorance, hallucination, delusion? All pain of the Soul is simply delusion.

The soul never changes in essence, but it is modified by Maya. Nature is God limited by mind. The evolution of nature is the modification of the soul. The soul in essence is the same in all forms of being. Its expression is modified by the body. This unity of soul, this common substance of humanity, is the basis of ethics and morality. In this sense all are one, and to hurt one's brother is to hurt one's Self.

Our bodies are symbols of thought behind, and the thoughts themselves are in their turn symbols of something behind them, that is, the one Real Existence, the Soul of our soul, the Self of the universe, the Life of our life, our true Self.

As long as we believe ourselves to be even the least different from God, fear remains with us; but when we know ourselves to be the One, fear goes: of what can we be afraid? By sheer force of will the Jnani rises beyond body, beyond mind, making this universe zero.

Thus he destroys Avidya and knows his true Self, the Atman. Happiness and misery are only in the senses, they cannot touch our real Self. The soul is beyond time, space, and causality — therefore unlimited, omnipresent.

Our goal is to perceive the Soul itself. We cannot perceive the Soul, because it has got mingled up with nature, with the mind, with the body. The ignorant man thinks his body is the Soul. The learned man thinks his mind is the Soul.

But both of them are mistaken. What makes the Soul get mingled up with all this? Different waves in the Chitta rise and cover the Soul; we only see a little reflection of the Soul through these waves; so, if the wave is one of anger, we see the Soul as angry; "I am angry," one says. If it is one of love, we see ourselves reflected in that wave, and say we are loving. If that wave is one of weakness, and the Soul is reflected in it, we think we are weak.

These various ideas come from these impressions, these Samskaras covering the Soul. The real nature of the Soul is not perceived as long as there is one single wave in the lake of the Chitta; this real nature will never be perceived until all the waves have subsided.

So, first, Patanjali teaches us the meaning of these waves; secondly, the best way to repress them; and thirdly, how to make one wave so strong as to suppress all other waves, fire eating fire as it were. When only one remains, it will be easy to suppress that also, and when that is gone, this Samadhi or concentration is called seedless. It leaves nothing, and the Soul is manifested just as It is, in Its own glory.

Then alone we know that the Soul is not a compound; It is the only eternal simple in the universe, and as such, It cannot be born, It cannot die; It is immortal, indestructible, the ever-living essence of intelligence.

The whole universe is really one. In speaking of the soul, to say that one is superior to another has no meaning. In speaking of the soul, to say that man is superior to the animal or the plant, has no meaning; the whole universe is one.

In plants the obstacle to soul-manifestation is very great; in animals a little less; and in man still less; in cultured, spiritual men still less; and in perfect men, it has vanished altogether. All our struggles, exercises, pains, pleasures, tears, and smiles, all that we do and think tend towards that goal, the tearing up of the screen, making the hole bigger, thinning the layers that remain between the manifestation and the reality behind.

Our work, therefore, is not to make the soul free, but to get rid of the bondages. The sun is covered by layers of clouds, but remains unaffected by them. The work of the wind is to drive the clouds away, and the more the clouds disappear, the more the light of the sun appears. There is no change whatsoever in the soul — Infinite, Absolute, Eternal, Knowledge, Bliss, and Existence.

Neither can there be birth or death for the soul. Dying, and being born, reincarnation, and going to heaven, cannot be for the soul. These are different appearances, different mirages, different dreams.

God is both the material and the efficient cause of this universe. If you say there is a God who is an infinite Being, and a soul which is also infinite, and a nature which is also infinite, you can go on multiplying infinites without limit which is simply absurd; you smash all logic. So God is both the material and the efficient cause of the universe; He projects this universe out of Himself.

Then how is it that God has become these walls and this table, that God has become the pig, and the murderer, and all the evil things in the world? We say that God is pure. How can He become all these degenerate things?

Our answer is: just as I am a soul and have a body, and in a sense, this body is not different from me, yet I, the real I, in fact, am not the body. For instance, I say, I am a child, a young man, or an old man, but my soul has not changed. It remains the same soul.

Similarly, the whole universe, comprising all nature and an infinite number of souls, is, as it were, the infinite body of God. He is interpenetrating the whole of it. He alone is unchangeable, but nature changes, and soul changes. He is unaffected by changes in nature and soul.

In what way does nature change? In its forms; it takes fresh forms. But the soul cannot change that way. The soul contracts and expands in knowledge. It contracts by evil deeds. Those deeds which contract the real natural knowledge and purity of the soul are called evil deeds. Those deeds, again, which bring out the natural glory of the soul, are called good deeds.

All these souls were pure, but they have become contracted; through the mercy of God, and by doing good deeds, they will expand and recover their natural purity. Everyone has the same chance, and in the long run, must get out. But this universe will not cease, because it is eternal.

There are God, soul, and nature, and soul and nature form the body of God, and, therefore, these three form one unit. It represents a higher stage of religious development and goes by the name of qualified monism. In dualism, the universe is conceived as a large machine set going by God while in qualified monism, it is conceived as an organism, interpenetrated by the Divine Self.

Find Happiness in Oneness

In some oil mills in India, bullocks are used that go round and round to grind the oil-seed. There is a yoke on the bullock's neck. They have a piece of wood protruding from the yoke, and on that is fastened a wisp of straw.

The bullock is blindfolded in such a way that it can only look forward, and so it stretches its neck to get at the straw; and in doing so, it pushes the piece of wood out a little further; and it makes another attempt with the same result, and yet another, and so on. It never catches the straw, but goes round and round in the hope of getting it, and in so doing, grinds out the oil.

In the same way you and I who are born slaves to nature, money and wealth, wives and children, are always chasing a wisp of straw, a mere chimera, and are going through an innumerable round of lives without obtaining what we seek. The great dream is love; we are all going to love and be loved, we are all going to be happy and never meet with misery, but the more we go towards happiness, the more it goes away from us.

Thus the world is going on, society goes on, and we, blinded slaves, have to pay for it without knowing. Study your own lives, and find how little of happiness there is in them, and how little in truth you have gained in the course of this wild-goose chase of the world.

Do you remember the story of Solon and Croesus? The king said to the great sage that Asia Minor was a very happy place. And the sage asked him, "Who is the happiest man? I have not seen anyone very happy."

"Nonsense," said Croesus, "I am the happiest man in the world."

"Wait, sir, till the end of your life; don't be in a hurry," replied the sage and went away.

In course of time that king was conquered by the Persians, and they ordered him to be burnt alive. The funeral pyre was prepared and when poor Croesus saw it, he cried aloud "Solon! Solon!" On being asked to whom he referred, he told his story, and the Persian emperor was touched, and saved his life.

Such is the life-story of each one of us; such is the tremendous power of nature over us. It repeatedly kicks us away, but still we pursue it with feverish excitement. We are always hoping against hope; this hope, this chimera maddens us; we are always hoping for happiness.

Utility is not the test of truth. Nevertheless, there is the highest utility in this. Happiness, we see is what everyone is seeking for, but the majority seek it in things which are evanescent and not real.

No happiness was ever found in the senses. There never was a person who found happiness in the senses or in enjoyment of the senses. Happiness is not in this heaven or in that heaven, it is in the soul; places do not signify anything.

Happiness is only found in the Spirit. Therefore the highest utility for mankind is to find this happiness in the Spirit.

Happiness presents itself before man, wearing the crown of sorrow on its head. He who welcomes it must also welcome sorrow.

We, we, and none else, are responsible for what we suffer. We are the effects, and we are the causes. We are free therefore. If I am unhappy, it has been of my own making, and that very thing shows that I can be happy if I will. If I am impure, that is also of my own making, and that very thing shows that I can be pure if I will. The human will stands beyond all circumstance. Before it — the strong, gigantic, infinite will and freedom in man — all the powers, even of nature, must bow down, succumb, and become its servants.

Can we do good to the world? In an absolute sense, no; in a relative sense, yes. No permanent or everlasting good can be done to the world; if it could be done, the world would not be this world. We may satisfy the hunger of a man for five minutes, but he will be hungry again. Every pleasure with which we supply a man may be seen to be momentary. No one can permanently cure this ever-recurring fever of pleasure and pain.

Can any permanent happiness be given to the world? In the ocean we cannot raise a wave without causing a hollow somewhere else. The sum total of the good things in the world has been the same throughout in its relation to man's need and greed. It cannot be increased or decreased.

Take the history of the human race as we know it today. Do we not find the same miseries and the same happiness, the same pleasures and pains, the same differences in position? Are not some rich, some poor, some high, some low, some healthy, some unhealthy?

All this was just the same with the Egyptians, the Greeks, and the Romans in ancient times as it is with the Americans today. So far as history is known, it has always been the same; yet at the same time we find that, running along with all these incurable differences of pleasure and pain, there has ever been the struggle to alleviate them. Every period of history has given birth to thousands of men and women who have worked hard to smooth the passage of life for others.

And how far have they succeeded? We can only play at driving the ball from one place to another. We take away pain from the physical plane, and it goes to the mental one. It is like that picture in Dante's hell where the misers were given a mass of gold to roll up a hill. Every time they rolled it up a little, it again rolled down.

All our talks about the millennium are very nice as schoolboys' stories, but they are no better than that. All nations that dream of the millennium also think that, of all peoples in the world, they will have the best of it then for themselves. This is the wonderfully unselfish idea of the millennium!

We are absolutely one; we are physically one, we are mentally one, and as spirit, it goes without saying, that we are one, if we believe in spirit at all. We are absolutely one; we are physically one, we are mentally one, and as spirit, it goes without saying, that we are one, if we believe in spirit at all.

But the scales are falling from our eyes, truth is beginning to manifest itself more and more, and that is a great gain to religion. The Self is the essence of this universe, the essence of all souls; He is the essence of your own life, nay, "Thou art That". You are one with this universe. He who says he is different from others, even by a hair's breadth, immediately becomes miserable.

Happiness belongs to him who knows this oneness, who knows he is one with this universe.

In this world we find that all happiness is followed by misery as its shadow.

Life has its shadow, death. They must go together, because they are not contradictory, not two separate existences, but different manifestations of the same unit, life and death, sorrow and happiness, good and evil.

The dualistic conception that good and evil are two separate entities, and that they are both going on eternally is absurd on the face of it. They are the diverse manifestations of one and the same fact, one time appearing as bad, and at another time as good. The difference does not exist in kind, but only in degree. They differ from each other in degree of intensity.

We find as a fact that the same nerve systems carry good and bad sensations alike, and when the nerves are injured, neither sensation comes to us. If a certain nerve is paralysed, we do not get the pleasurable feelings that used to come along that wires and at the same time we do not get the painful feelings either. They are never two, but the same.

Again, the same thing produces pleasure and pain at different times of life. The same phenomenon will produce pleasure in one, and pain in another. The eating of meat produces pleasure to a man, but pain to the animal which is eaten. There has never been anything which gives pleasure to all alike. Some are pleased, others displeased. So on it will go. Therefore, this duality of existence is denied.

There was a great king in ancient India who was once asked four questions, of which one was: "What is the most wonderful thing in the world?" "Hope," was the answer.

This is the most wonderful thing. Day and nights we see people dying around us, and yet we think we shall not die; we never think that we shall die, or that we shall suffer. Each man thinks that success will be his, hoping against hope, against all odds, against all mathematical reasoning.

Nobody is ever really happy here. If a man be wealthy and have plenty to eat, his digestion is: out of order, and he cannot eat. If a man's digestion be good, and he have the digestive power of a cormorant, he has nothing to put into his mouth. If he be rich, he has no children. If he be hungry and poor, he has a whole regiment of children, and does not know what to do with them.

Why is it so? Because happiness and misery are the obverse and reverse of the same coin; he who takes happiness, must take misery also. We all have this foolish idea that we can have happiness without misery, and it has taken such possession of us that we have no control over the senses.

The Vedanta system begins with tremendous pessimism, and ends with real optimism. We deny the sense-optimism but assert the real optimism of the Supersensuous. That real happiness is not in the senses but above the senses; and it is in every man. The sort of optimism which we see in the world is what will lead to ruin through the senses.

The ideal of happiness, that which brings man more happiness, is of greater utility to him than these higher things which do not improve his material conditions or bring him such great happiness. All the sciences are for this one end, to bring happiness to humanity; and that which brings the larger amount of happiness, man takes and gives up that which brings a lesser amount of happiness.

We have seen how happiness is either in the body, or in the mind, or in the Atman. With animals, and in the lowest human beings who are very much like animals, happiness is all in the body. No man can eat with the same pleasure as a famished dog or a wolf; so in the dog and the wolf the happiness is entirely in the body. In men we find a higher plane of happiness, that of thought; and in the Jnani there is the highest plane of happiness in the Self, the Atman.

So to the philosopher this knowledge of the Self is of the highest utility, because it gives him the highest happiness possible. Sense-gratifications or physical things cannot be of the highest utility to him, because he does not find in them the same pleasure that he finds in knowledge itself; and after all, knowledge is the one goal and is really the highest happiness that we know. All who work in ignorance are, as it were, the draught animals of the Devas.

The word Deva is here used in the sense of a wise man. All the people that work and toil and labour like machines do not really enjoy life, but it is the wise man who enjoys. A rich man buys a picture at a cost of a hundred thousand dollars perhaps, but it is the man who understands art that enjoys it; and if the rich man is without knowledge of art, it is useless to him, he is only the owner. All over the world, it is the wise man who enjoys the happiness of the world. The ignorant man never enjoys; he has to work for others unconsciously.

Never producing pain by thought, word, and deed, in any living being, is what is called Ahimsa, non-injury. There is no virtue higher than non-injury. There is no happiness higher than what a man obtains by this attitude of non-offensiveness, to all creation.

"He jests at scars that never felt a wound."

I tell you it is nothing of the kind. If it is happiness to enjoy the consciousness of this small body, it must be greater happiness to enjoy the consciousness of two bodies, the measure of happiness increasing with the consciousness of an increasing number of bodies, the aim, the ultimate of happiness being reached when it would become a universal consciousness.

Therefore, to gain this infinite universal individuality, this miserable little prison-individuality must go. Then alone can death cease when I am alone with life, then alone can misery cease when I am one with happiness itself, then alone can all errors cease when I am one with knowledge itself; and this is the necessary scientific conclusion.

Science has proved to me that physical individuality is a delusion, that really my body is one little continuously changing body in an unbroken ocean of matter; and Advaita (unity) is the necessary conclusion with my other counterpart, soul.

We cannot add happiness to this world; similarly, we cannot add pain to it either. The sum total of the energies of pleasure and pain displayed here on earth will be the same throughout. We just push it from this side to the other side, and from that side to this, but it will remain the same, because to remain so is its very nature.

This ebb and flow, this rising and falling, is in the world's very nature; it would be as logical to hold otherwise as to say that we may have life without death. This is complete nonsense, because the very idea of life implies death and the very idea of pleasure implies pain. The lamp is constantly burning out, and that is its life. If you want to have life, you have to die every moment for it.

Life and death are only different expressions of the same thing looked at from different standpoints; they are the falling and the rising of the same wave, and the two form one whole. One looks at the "fall" side and becomes a pessimist another looks at the "rise" side and becomes an optimist.

When a boy is going to school and his father and mother are taking care of him, everything seems blessed to him; his wants are simple, he is a great optimist. But the old man, with his varied experience, becomes calmer and is sure to have his warmth considerably cooled down. So, old nations, with signs of decay all around them, are apt to be less hopeful than new nations.

There is a proverb in India: "A thousand years a city, and a thousand years a forest." This change of city into forest and vice versa is going on everywhere, and it makes people optimists or pessimists according to the side they see of it.

You have all heard of that rich man in Rome who learnt one day that he had only about a million pounds of his property left; he said, "What shall I do tomorrow?" and forthwith committed suicide. A million pounds was poverty to him.

What is joy, and what is sorrow? It is a vanishing quantity, continually vanishing. When I was a child I thought if I could be a cabman, it would be the very acme of happiness for me to drive about. I do not think so now.

To what joy will you cling? This is the one point we must all try to understand, and it is one of the last superstitions to leave us.

Everyone's idea of pleasure is different. I have seen a man who is not happy unless he swallows a lump of opium every day. He may dream of a heaven where the land is made of opium. That would be a very bad heaven for me.

Again and again in Arabian poetry we read of heaven with beautiful gardens, through which rivers run. I lived much of my life in a country where there is too much water; many villages are flooded and thousands of lives are sacrificed every year. So, my heaven would not have gardens through which rivers flow; I would have a land where very little rain falls.

Our pleasures are always changing. If a young man dreams of heaven, he dreams of a heaven where he will have a beautiful wife. When that same man becomes old he does not want a wife. It is our necessities which make our heaven, and the heaven changes with the change of our necessities.

If we had a heaven like that desired by those to whom sense-enjoyment is the very end of existence, then we would not progress. That would be the most terrible curse we could pronounce on the soul.

Is this all we can come to? A little weeping and dancing, and then to die like a dog! What a curse you pronounce on the head of humanity when you long for these things! That is what you do when you cry after the joys of this world, for you do not know what true joy is.

What philosophy insists on is not to give up joys, but to know what joy really is. The Norwegian heaven is a tremendous fighting place where they all sit before Odin; they have a wild boar hunt, and then they go to war and slash each other to pieces. But in some way or other, after a few hours of such fighting, the wounds are all healed up, and they go into a hall where the boar has been roasted, and have a carousal. And then the wild boar takes form again, ready to be hunted the next day.

That is much the same thing as our heaven, not a whit worse, only our ideas may be a little more refined. We want to hunt wild boars, and get to a place where all enjoyments will continue, just as the Norwegian imagines that the wild boar is hunted and eaten every day, and recovers the next day.

Now, philosophy insists that there is a joy which is absolute, which never changes. That joy cannot be the joys and pleasures we have in this life, and yet Vedanta shows that everything that is joyful in this life is but a particle of that real joy, because that is the only joy there is. Every moment really we are enjoying the absolute bliss, though covered up, misunderstood, and caricatured. Wherever there is any blessing, blissfulness, or joy, even the joy of the thief in stealing, it is that absolute bliss coming out, only it has become obscured, muddled up, as it were, with all sorts of extraneous conditions, and misunderstood.

But to understand that, we have to go through the negation, and then the positive side will begin. We have to give up ignorance and all that is false, and then truth will begin to reveal itself to us. When we have grasped the truth, things which we gave up at first will take new shape and form, will appear to us in a new light, and become deified. They will have become sublimated, and then we shall understand them in their true light. But to understand them, we have first to get a glimpse of truth; we must give them up at first, and then we get them back again, deified. We have to give up all our miseries and sorrows, all our little joys.

When I was in Boston, a young man came up to me, and gave me a scrap of paper on which he had written a name and address, followed by these words: "All the wealth and all the happiness of the world are yours, if you only know how to get them. If you come to me, I will teach you how to get them. Charge, $5."

He gave me this and said, "What do you think of this?" I said, "Young man, why don't you get the money to print this? You have not even enough money to get this printed!"

He did not understand this. He was infatuated with the idea that he could get immense wealth and happiness without any trouble.

There are two extremes into which men are running; one is extreme optimism, when everything is rosy and nice and good; the other, extreme pessimism, when everything seems to be against them. The majority of men have more or less undeveloped brains. One in a million we see with a well-developed brain; the rest either have peculiar idiosyncrasies, or are monomaniacs.

The Secret to True Success

No need of looking behind. FORWARD! We want infinite energy, infinite zeal, infinite courage, and infinite patience, then only will great things be achieved.

Do not figure out big plans at first, but begin slowly, feel your ground, and proceed up and up.

Never mind the struggles, the mistakes. I never heard a cow tell a lie, but it is only a cow— never a man. So never mind these failures, these little backslidings; hold the ideal thousand times, and if you fail a thousand times, make the attempt once more.

Start with the idea that we can finish all experience in this world, in this incarnation. We must aim to become perfect in this life, this very moment. Success only comes to that life amongst men who wants to do this, this very moment. It is acquired by him who says, "Faith, I wait upon faith come what may". Therefore, go on knowing you are to finish this very moment. Struggle hard and then if you do not succeed, you are not to blame. Let the world praise or blame you. Let all the wealth of the earth come to your feet, or let you be made the poorest on earth. Let death come this moment or hundreds of years hence. Swerve not from the path you have taken. All good thoughts are immortal and go to make Buddhas and Christs.

Go on bravely. Do not expect success in a day or a year. Always hold on to the highest. Be steady. Avoid jealousy and selfishness. Be obedient and eternally faithful to the causes of truth, humanity, and your country, and you will move the world. Remember it is the person, the life, which is the secret of power— nothing else.

Every successful man must have behind him somewhere tremendous integrity, tremendous sincerity, and that is the cause of his signal success in life. He may not have been perfectly unselfish; yet he was tending towards it. If he had been perfectly unselfish, his would have been as great a success as that of the Buddha or of the Christ. The degree of unselfishness marks the degree of success everywhere.

Go on bravely — never mind about designs and other details at present — "With the horse will come the reins". Work unto death — I am with you, and when I am gone, my spirit will work with you. This life comes and goes — wealth, fame, enjoyments are only of a few days. It is better, far better to die on the field of duty, preaching the truth, than to die like a worldly worm. Advance!

Neither numbers nor powers nor wealth nor learning nor anything else will prevail, but purity, living the life, in one word, anubhuti, realisation. Let there be a dozen such lion-souls in each country, lions who have broken their own bonds, who have touched the infinite, whose whole soul is gone to Brahman, who care neither for wealth nor power nor fame, and these will be enough to shake the world.

Persevere on, my brave lads. We have only just begun. Never despond! Never say enough!

One of the greatest lessons I have learnt in my life is to pay as much attention to the means of work as to its end. He was a great man from whom I learnt it, and his own life was a practical demonstration of this great principle I have been always learning great lessons from that one principle, and it appears to me that all the secret of success is there; to pay as much attention to the means as to the end.

The man who says that he will work when the world has become all good and then he will enjoy bliss is as likely to succeed as the man who sits beside the Ganga and says, "I will ford the river when all the water has run into the ocean."

Be moral. Be brave. Be a heart-whole man. Strictly moral, brave unto desperation.

Be of good cheer and believe that we are selected by the Lord to do great things, and we will do them.

We would do nothing ourselves and would scoff at others who try to do something— this is the bane that has brought our downfall as a nation. Want of sympathy and lack of energy are at the root of all misery, and you must therefore give these two up. Who but the Lord knows what potentialities there are in particular individuals— let all have opportunities, and leave the rest to the Lord. It is indeed very difficult to have an equal love for all, but without it there is nomukti.

Say, "This misery that I am suffering is of my own doing, and that very thing proves that it will have to be undone by me alone." That which I created, I can demolish… Therefore stand up, be bold, be strong, Take the whole responsibility on your own shoulders, and know that you are the creator of your destiny. All the strength and succour you want is within yourself.

No great work can be achieved by humbug. It is through love, a passion for truth, and tremendous energy, that all undertakings are accomplished.

I want each one of my children to be a hundred times greater than I could ever be. Everyone of you must be a giant—must, that is my word. Obedience, readiness, and love for the cause— if you have these three, nothing can hold you back.

Listen to an old story. A lazy tramp sauntering along the road saw an old man sitting at the door of his house and stopped to inquire of him the whereabouts of a certain place.

"How far is such and such a village?" he asked.

The old man remained silent. The man repeated his query several times. Still there was no answer. Disgusted at this, the traveller turned to go away.

The old man then stood up and said, "The village of — is only a mile from here."

"What!" said the tramp, "Why did you not speak when I asked you before?"

"Because then", said the old man, "you seemed so halting and careless about proceeding, but now you are starting off in good earnest, and you have a right to an answer."

Will you remember this story, my son? Go to work, the rest will come: "Whosoever not trusting in anything else but Me, rests on Me, I supply him with everything he needs" (Gita, IX. 22). This is no dream.

Cowardice is Weakness

Always keep the mind cheerful. Everyone will die once. Cowards suffer the pangs of death again and again, solely due to the fear in their own minds.

Fear never leaves those who earn their livelihoods by unethical means or who cause harm to others. Therefore, at this time when we face the great fear of death, desist from all such behaviour.

Bear in mind, my children, that only cowards and those who are weak commit sin and tell lies. The brave are always moral. Try to be moral, try to be brave, try to be sympathising.

Know that talking ill of others in private is a sin. You must wholly avoid it. Many things may occur to the mind, but it gradually makes a mountain of a molehill if you try to express them. Everything is ended if you forgive and forget.

If you read the Vedas, you will find this word always repeated — fearlessness — fear nothing. Fear is a sign of weakness. A man must go about his duties without taking notice of the sneers and the ridicule of the world.

When these cardinal virtues will be manifested in you, then only you will be able to work with great energy. Otherwise, mere taking the name of the Guru will not do. Never shall you be able to know anything if you persist in pleading ignorance. We want something of a higher tone — that will appeal to the intellect of the learned. It won't do merely to get up musical parties and all that. Not only will this festival be his memorial, but also the central union of an intense propaganda of his doctrines. All will come in good time. But at times I fret and stamp like a leashed hound. Onward and forward, my old watchword. I am doing well. No use going back to India in a hurry. Summon all your energies and set yourselves to work heart and soul; that will really be heroic.

Once when I was in Varanasi, I was passing through a place where there was a large tank of water on one side and a high wall on the other. It was in the grounds where there were many monkeys.

The monkeys of Varanasi are huge brutes and are sometimes surly. They now took it into their heads not to allow me to pass through their street, so they howled and shrieked and clutched at my feet as I passed.

As they pressed closer, I began to run, but the faster I ran, the faster came the monkeys and they began to bite at me. It seemed impossible to escape, but just then I met a stranger who called out to me, "Face the brutes." I turned and faced the monkeys, and they fell back and finally fled.

That is a lesson for all life — face the terrible, face it boldly. Like the monkeys, the hardships of life fall back when we cease to flee before them. If we are ever to gain freedom, it must be by conquering nature, never by running away. Cowards never win victories. We have to fight fear and troubles and ignorance if we expect them to flee before us.

What is death? What are terrors? Do you not see the Lord's face in them? Fly from evil and terror and misery, and they will follow you. Face them, and they will flee. The whole world worships ease and pleasure, and very few dare to worship that which is painful.

To rise above both is the idea of freedom. Unless man passes through this gate he cannot be free.

We all have to face these. We strive to worship the Lord, but the body rises between, nature rises between Him and us and blinds our vision. We must learn how to worship and love Him in the thunderbolt, in shame, in sorrow, in sin. All the world has ever been preaching the God of virtue.

I preach a God of virtue and a God of sin in one. Take Him if you dare — that is the one way to salvation; then alone will come to us the Truth Ultimate which comes from the idea of oneness. Then will be lost the idea that one is greater than another.

The nearer we approach the law of freedom, the more we shall come under the Lord, and troubles will vanish. Then we shall not differentiate the door of hell from the gate of heaven, nor differentiate between men and say, "I am greater than any being in the universe."

Until we see nothing in the world but the Lord Himself, all these evils will beset us and we shall make all these distinctions; because it is only in the Lord, in the Spirit, that we are all one; and until we see God everywhere, this unity will not exist for us.

Be brave. Be a heart-whole man. Strictly moral, brave unto desperation. Die in obeying commands like a soldier, and go to Nirvana, but no cowardice.

Don't bother your head with religious theories. Cowards only sin, brave men never, no, not even in mind. Try to love anybody and everybody. Be a man and try to make those immediately under your care, namely Ram, Krishnamayi, and Indu, brave, moral, and sympathising.

No religion for you, my children, but morality and bravery. No cowardice, no sin, no crime, no weakness — the rest will come of itself.

There is success and failure in every work. But I am inclined to believe that one who is a coward will be born after death as an insect or a worm, that there is no salvation for a coward even after millions of years of penance.

The moment you fear, you are nobody. It is fear that is the great cause of misery in the world. It is fear that is the greatest of all superstitions. It is fear that is the cause of our woes, and it is fearlessness that brings heaven even in a moment.

If you are really my children, you will fear nothing, stop at nothing. You will be like lions. We must rouse India and the whole world. No cowardice. I will take no nay.

Money is the only God of many beings. Weak men, when they lose everything and feel themselves weak, try all sorts of uncanny methods of making money, and come to astrology and all these things. "It is the coward and the fool who says, 'This is fate'" — so says the Sanskrit proverb. But it is the strong man who stands up and says, "I will make my fate." It is people who are getting old who talk of fate.

Courage! Everything will come about by degrees. From all of you I want this that you must discard for ever self-aggrandisement, faction-mongering, and jealousy. You must be all-forbearing, like Mother Earth. If you can achieve this, the world will be at your feet.

Brave, bold men, these are what we want. What we want is vigour in the blood, strength in the nerves, iron muscles and nerves of steel, not softening namby-pamby ideas. Avoid all these. Avoid all mystery.

Stand up and be strong! No fear. No superstition. Face the truth as it is! If death comes — that is the worst of our miseries — let it come! We are determined to die game.

Stand and die in your own strength, if there is any sin in the world, it is weakness; avoid all weakness, for weakness is sin, weakness is death.

Strength, strength it is that we want so much in this life, for what we call sin and sorrow have all one cause, and that is our weakness. With weakness comes ignorance, and with ignorance comes misery.

Manifest Your Inward Power

Whatever you believe, that you will be. If you believe yourselves to be sages, sages you will be tomorrow. There is nothing to obstruct you.

For if there is one common doctrine that runs through all our apparently fighting and contradictory sects, it is that all glory, power, and purity are within the soul already; only according to Ramanuja, the soul contracts and expands at times, and according to Shankara, it comes under a delusion. Never mind these differences. All admit the truth that the power is there — potential or manifest it is there — and the sooner you believe that, the better for you.

All power is within you; you can do anything and everything. Believe in that; do not believe that you are weak; do not believe that you are half-crazy lunatics as most of us believe now-a-days. You can do anything and everything, without even the guidance of any one.

All the powers in the universe are already ours. It is we who have put our hands before our eyes and cry that it is dark. Know that there is no darkness around us. Take the hands away and there is the light which was from the beginning. Darkness never existed, weakness never existed. We who are fools cry that we are weak; we who are fools cry that we are impure.

Advance like a hero. Don't be thwarted by anything. How many days will this body last, with its happiness and misery? When you have got the human body, then rouse the Atman within and say — I have reached the state of fearlessness! Say — I am the Atman in which my lower ego has become merged for ever.

Be perfect in this idea; and then as long as the body endures, speak unto others this message of fearlessness: "Thou art That", "Arise, awake, and stop not till the goal is reached!" If you can achieve this, then shall I know that you are really a tenacious East Bengal man.

If there is sincerity of spirit, I tell you, for a certainty, you will attain self-realization in this very life. But manly endeavour is wanted. Do you know what it is? "I shall certainly attain Self-knowledge. Whatever obstacles may come, I shall certainly overcome them" — a firm determination like this is Purushakara.

"Whether my mother, father, friends, brothers, wife, and children live or die, whether this body remains or goes, I shall never turn back till I attain to the vision of the Atman" — this resolute endeavour to advance towards one's goal, setting at naught all other considerations, is termed manly endeavour.

Otherwise, endeavour for creature comforts even beasts and birds show. Man has got this body simply to realise Self-knowledge. If you follow the common run of people in the world and float with the general current, where then is your manliness? Well, the common people are going to the jaws of death! But you have come to conquer it!

All great undertakings are achieved through mighty obstacles. — You valiant one, put forth your manly efforts; Wretched people under the grip of lust and gold deserve to be looked upon with indifference.

Apply to the service of the Lord that active impulse of manliness which your eagerness to help me through brotherly love has brought out in you. Do not open out your mind, unless you feel it will be positively beneficial. Use agreeable and wholesome language towards even the greatest enemy.

The desire for fame, for riches, for enjoyment is quite natural to every mortal, dear brother, and if that agrees well with serving both ways (i.e. serving both God and mammon), why, all men would exhibit great zeal! It is only the great saint who can work, making a mountain of an atom of virtue in others and cherishing no desire but that of the good of the world

All knowledge is within us. All perfection is there already in the soul. But this perfection has been covered up by nature; layer after layer of nature is covering this purity of the soul. What have we to do? Really we do not develop our souls at all. What can develop the perfect? We simply take the evil off; and the soul manifests itself in its pristine purity, its natural, innate freedom.

All noble undertakings are fraught with obstacles. It is quite in the nature of things. Keep up the deepest mental poise. Take not even the slightest notice of what puerile creatures may be saying against you. Indifference, indifference, indifference!

All search is vain, until we begin to perceive that knowledge is within ourselves, that no one can help us, that we must help ourselves.

All the misery we have is of our own choosing; such is our nature. The old Chinaman, who having been kept in prison for sixty years was released on the coronation of a new emperor, exclaimed, when he came out, that he could not live; he must go back to his horrible dungeon among the rats and mice; he could not bear the light. So he asked them to kill him or send him back to the prison, and he was sent back.

Exactly similar is the condition of all men. We run headlong after all sorts of misery, and are unwilling to be freed from them. Every day we run after pleasure, and before we reach it, we find it is gone, it has slipped through our fingers. Still we do not cease from our mad pursuit, but on and on we go, blinded fools that we are.

Vedanta not only insists that the ideal is practical, but that it has been so all the time; and this Ideal, this Reality, is our own nature. Everything else that you see is false, untrue. As soon as you say, "I am a little mortal being," you are saying something which is not true, you are giving the lie to yourselves, you are hypnotising yourselves into something vile and weak and wretched.

The Vedanta recognises no sin, it only recognises error. And the greatest error, says the Vedanta, is to say that you are weak, that you are a sinner, a miserable creature, and that you have no power and you cannot do this and that. Every time you think in that way, you, as it were, rivet one more link in the chain that binds you down, you add one more layer of hypnotism on to your own soul.

Therefore, whosoever thinks he is weak is wrong, whosoever thinks he is impure is wrong, and is throwing a bad thought into the world. This we must always bear in mind that in the Vedanta there is no attempt at reconciling the present life — the hypnotised life, this false life which we have assumed — with the ideal; but this false life must go, and the real life which is always existing must manifest itself, must shine out.

No man becomes purer and purer, it is a matter of greater manifestation. The veil drops away, and the native purity of the soul begins to manifest itself. Everything is ours already — infinite purity, freedom, love, and power.

The Vedanta also says that not only can this be realised in the depths of forests or caves, but by men in all possible conditions of life. We have seen that the people who discovered these truths were neither living in caves nor forests, nor following the ordinary vocations of life, but men who, we have every reason to believe, led the busiest of lives, men who had to command armies, to sit on thrones, and look to the welfare of millions — and all these, in the days of absolute monarchy, and not as in these days when a king is to a great extent a mere figurehead.

Yet they could find time to think out all these thoughts, to realise them, and to teach them to humanity. How much more then should it be practical for us whose lives, compared with theirs, are lives of leisure? That we cannot realise them is a shame to us, seeing that we are comparatively free all the time, having very little to do.

My requirements are as nothing compared with those of an ancient absolute monarch. My wants are as nothing compared with the demands of Arjuna on the battlefield of Kurukshetra, commanding a huge army; and yet he could find time in the midst of the din and turmoil of battle to talk the highest philosophy and to carry it into his life also. Surely we ought to be able to do as much in this life of ours — comparatively free, easy, and comfortable.

Most of us here have more time than we think we have, if we really want to use it for good. With the amount of freedom we have we can attain to two hundred ideals in this life, if we will, but we must not degrade the ideal to the actual.

One of the most insinuating things comes to us in the shape of persons who apologise for our mistakes and teach us how to make special excuses for all our foolish wants and foolish desires; and we think that their ideal is the only ideal we need have. But it is not so. The Vedanta teaches no such thing. The actual should be reconciled to the ideal, the present life should be made to coincide with life eternal.

"Arise, awake, sleep no more; within each of you there is the power to remove all wants and all miseries. Believe this, and that power will be manifested.

Avoid weakness and slavery

Look at the "ocean" and not at the "wave"; see no difference between ant and angel. Every worm is the brother of the Nazarene. How say one is greater and one less? Each is great in his own place.

We are in the sun and in the stars as much as here. Spirit is beyond space and time and is everywhere. Every mouth praising the Lord is my mouth, every eye seeing is my eye.

We are confined nowhere; we are not body, the universe is our body. We are magicians waving magic wands and creating scenes before us at will. We are the spider in his huge web, who can go on the varied strands wheresoever he desires. The spider is now only conscious of the spot where he is, but he will in time become conscious of the whole web.

We are now conscious only where the body is, we can use only one brain; but when we reach ultraconsciousness, we know all, we can use all brains. Even now we can "give the push" in consciousness, and it goes beyond and acts in the superconscious.

We are striving "to be" and nothing more, no "I" ever — just pure crystal, reflecting all, but ever the same, When that state is reached, there is no more doing; the body becomes a mere mechanism, pure without care for it; it cannot become impure.

Know you are the Infinite, then fear must die. Say ever, "I and my Father are one."

Awake, awake, great ones! The world is burning with misery. Can you sleep? Let us call and call till the sleeping gods awake, till the god within answers to the call. What more is in life? What greater work? The details come to me as I go. I never make plans. Plans grow and work themselves. I only say, awake, awake!

Be brave and be sincere; then follow any path with devotion, and you must reach the Whole. Once lay hold of one link of the chain, and the whole chain must come by degrees.

Be free; hope for nothing from anyone. I am sure if you look back upon your lives you will find that you were always vainly trying to get help from others which never came.

Be perfectly unselfish, be steady and work on. We will do great things; do not fear… One thing more. Be the servant of all, and do not try in the least to govern others. That will excite jealousy and destroy everything… Go on. You have worked wonderfully well. We do not wait for help, we will work it out, my boy, be self-reliant, faithful and patient. Do not antagonise my other friends, live in harmony with all. My eternal love to all.

Be perfectly resigned, perfectly unconcerned; then alone can you do any true work. No eyes can see the real forces; we can only see the results. Put out self, forget it; just let God work, it is His business.

Being reminded of weakness does not help much; give strength, and strength does not come by thinking of weakness all the time. The remedy for weakness is not brooding over weakness, but thinking of strength.

Blame neither man, nor God, nor anyone in the world. When you find yourselves suffering, blame yourselves, and try to do better.

Calm and silent and steady work, and no newspaper humbug, no name-making, you must always remember.

Come out into the broad light of day, come out from the little narrow paths, for how can the infinite soul rest content to live and die in small ruts?

Each one of us reaps what we ourselves have sown. These miseries under which we suffer, these bondages under which we struggle, have been caused by ourselves, and none else in the universe is to blame. God is the least to blame for it.

Each person tries to hold himself faultless and lay the blame upon somebody or something else, or even on bad luck.

Even at the gate of death, in the greatest danger, in the thick of the battlefield, at the bottom of the ocean, on the tops of the highest mountains, in the thickest of the forest, tell yourself, "I am He, I am He". Day and night say, "I am He". It is the greatest strength; it is religion.

Help does not come from without; it comes from within ourselves. Cry to all the gods in the universe. I cried for years, and in the end I found that I was helped. But help came from within.

It is fear alone that is death. You have to go beyond all fear. So from this day be fearless.

Let people say whatever they like, stick to your own convictions, and rest assured, the world will be at your feet. They say, 'Have faith in this fellow or that fellow', but, I say, 'Have faith in yourself first'. that's the way.

Let us be true. Nine-tenths of our life's energy is spent in trying to make people think us that which we are not. That energy would be more rightly spent in becoming that which we would like to be.

Let us proclaim to every soul: उत्तिष्ठत जाग्रत प्राप्य वरान्निबोधत — Arise, awake, and stop not till the goal is reached. Arise, awake! Awake from this hypnotism of weakness.

Mark you, let us all be honest. If we cannot follow the ideal, let us confess our weakness, but not degrade it; let not any try to pull it down.

No great thing can be done without sacrifice.

Nobody will come to help you if you put yourself forward as a leader. Kill self first if you want to succeed.

Nothing else is necessary but these — love, sincerity, and patience.

Persevere on, my brave lads, We have only just begun. Never despond! Never say enough!

So'ham — I am He. Repeat the idea constantly, voluntarily at first; then it becomes automatic in practice. It percolates to the nerves. So this idea, by rote, by repetition, should be driven even into the nerves.

Struggle hard and then if you do not succeed, you are not to blame. Let the world praise or blame you. Let all the wealth of the earth come to your feet, or let you be made the poorest on earth. Let death come this moment or hundreds of years hence. Swerve not from the path you have taken. All good thoughts are immortal and go to make Buddhas and Christs.

Struggle, struggle, was my motto for the last ten years. Struggle, still say I. When it was all dark, I used to say, struggle; when light is breaking in, I still say, struggle. Be not afraid, my children. Look not up in that attitude of fear towards that infinite starry vault as if it would crush you.

Take care! Beware of everything that is untrue; stick to truth and we shall succeed, maybe slowly, but surely.

Take courage and work on. Patience and steady work — this is the only way. Go on; remember — patience and purity and courage and steady work. . . . So long as you are pure, and true to your principles, you will never fail.

Take up one idea. Make that one idea your life — think of it, dream of it, live on that idea. Let the brain, muscles, nerves, every part of your body, be full of that idea, and just leave every other idea alone. This is the way to success.

The brave alone can afford to be sincere. Compare the lion and the fox.

The whole secret of existence is to have no fear. Never fear what will become of you.

This is the first lesson to learn: be determined not to curse anything outside, not to lay the blame upon any one outside, but be a man, stand up, lay the blame on yourself. You will find, that is always true. Get hold of yourself.

Those who die, merely suffering the woes of life like cats and dogs, are they men? He is a man who even when agitated by the sharp interaction of pleasure and pain is discriminating, and knowing them to be of an evanescent nature, becomes passionately devoted to the Atman. This is all the difference between men and animals.

Truth, purity, and unselfishness — wherever these are present, there is no power below or above the sun to crush the possessor thereof. Equipped with these, one individual is able to face the whole universe in opposition.

We are forever trying to make our weakness look like strength, our sentiment like love, our cowardice like courage, etc. Say to your soul in regard to vanities, weaknesses, etc., "This does not befit thee. This does not befit thee".

Whatever you believe, that you will be. If you believe yourselves to be sages, sages you will be tomorrow. There is nothing to obstruct you.

You are a part of the Infinite. This is your nature. Hence you are your brother's keeper… When you hurt anyone you hurt yourself, for you and your brother are one.

You have to grow from the inside out. None can teach you, none can make you spiritual. There is no other teacher but your own soul.

You must have an iron will if you would cross the ocean. You must be strong enough to pierce mountains.

Be free; hope for nothing from anyone. I am sure if you look back upon your lives you will find that you were always vainly trying to get help from others which never came.

Be not afraid, for all great power throughout the history of humanity has been with the people. From out of their ranks have come all the greatest geniuses of the world, and history can only repeat itself. Be not afraid of anything. You will do marvellous work.

Be not in despair, the way is very difficult, like walking on the edge of a razor; yet despair not, arise, awake, and find the ideal, the goal.

Be strong, my young friends; that is my advice to you. You will be nearer to Heaven through football than through the study of the Gita. These are bold words; but I have to say them, for I love you. I know where the shoe pinches.

Calm and silent and steady work, and no newspaper humbug, no name-making, you must always remember.

Come out into the broad open light of day, come out from the little narrow paths, for how can the infinite soul rest content to live and die in small ruts? Come out into the universe of Light. Everything in the universe is yours, stretch out your arms and embrace it with love. If you ever felt you wanted to do that, you have felt God.

Cowards only sin, brave men never, no, not even in mind.

Do not be afraid of a small beginning. great things come afterwards. Be courageous. Do not try to lead your brethren, but serve them. The brutal mania for leading has sunk many a great ships in the waters of life. Take care especially of that, i.e. be unselfish even unto death, and work.

Do not figure out big plans at first, but, begin slowly, feel your ground and proceed up and up.

Do not wait for anybody or anything. Do whatever you can. Build your hope on none.

Go on bravely. Do not expect success in a day or a year. Always hold on to the highest. Be steady. Avoid jealousy and selfishness. Be obedient and eternally faithful to the cause of truth, humanity, and your country, and you will move the world.

Have faith in yourselves, and stand up on that faith and be strong; that is what we need.

Hold on to your own ideal. . . . Above all, never attempt to guide or rule others, or, as the Yankees say, "boss" others. Be the servant of all.

I hate cowardice; I will have nothing to do with cowards or political nonsense. I do not believe in any politics. God and truth are the only politics in the world, everything else is trash.

I want each one of my children to be a hundred times greater than I could ever be. Everyone of you must be a giant— must, that is my word. Obedience, readiness, and love for the cause— if you have these three, nothing can hold you back.

If you are really my children, you will fear nothing, stop at nothing. You will be like lions. We must rouse India and the whole world. No cowardice. I will take no nay. Do you understand?

If you can think that infinite power, infinite knowledge and indomitable energy lie within you, and if you can bring out that power, you also can become like me.

Infinite patience, infinite purity, and infinite perseverance are the secret of success in a good cause.

It is our own mental attitude which makes the world what it is for us. Our thoughts make things beautiful, our thoughts make things ugly. The whole world is in our own minds. Learn to see things in the proper light.

Know that every time you feel weak, you not only hurt yourself but also the cause. Infinite faith and strength are the only conditions of success.

Let people say whatever they like, stick to your own convictions, and rest assured, the world will be at your feet. They say, 'Have faith in this fellow or that fellow', but, I say, 'Have faith in yourself first'. that's the way.

We are responsible for what we are, and whatever we wish ourselves to be, we have the power to make ourselves. If what we are now has been the result of our own past actions, it certainly follows that whatever we wish to be in future can be produced by our present actions; so we have to know how to act.

We are what our thoughts have made us; so take care about what you think. Words are secondary. Thoughts live; they travel far.

We reap what we sow. We are the makers of our own fate. None else has the blame, none has the praise.

Whatever you think, that you will be. If you think yourselves weak, weak you will be; if you think yourselves strong, strong you will be; if you think yourselves impure, impure you will be; if you think yourselves pure, pure you will be.

Blame none for your own faults, stand upon your own feet, and take the whole responsibility upon yourselves. Say, "This misery that I am suffering is of my own doing, and that very thing proves that it will have to be undone by me alone." That which I created, I can demolish; that which is created by some one else I shall never be able to destroy. Therefore, stand up, be bold, be strong. Take the whole responsibility on your own shoulders, and know that you are the creator of your own destiny.

Bold words and bolder deeds are what we want. Awake, awake, great ones! The world is burning with misery. Can you sleep? Let us call and call till the sleeping gods awake, till the god within answers to the call. What more is in life? What greater work? The details come to me as I go. I never make plans. Plans grow and work themselves. I only say, awake, awake!

The mission of the Institute of Thought and Philosophy is to preserve and propagate the teachings of Swami Vivekananda. This great Indian spiritual leader is known for introducing the West to Hinduism. Drawing from his vast literary legacy, we provide valuable insights and practical guidance for modern living.

Have any query or feedback? Please reach out to us at ITPPress123@gmail.com